Advance Praise for *China's War on Faith*

"*China's War on Faith* is a matter of national security for every American and every person of faith around the world."

—Mike Pompeo, former Secretary of State

CHINA'S WAR ON FAITH

SAM BROWNBACK
with MICHAEL ARKUSH

A REPUBLIC BOOK
ISBN: 978-1-64572-113-0
ISBN (eBook): 978-1-64572-114-7

China's War on Faith

Cover Design by Jim Villaflores

Republic Book Publishers
New York, NY
www.republicbookpublishers.com

Published in the United States of America
1 2 3 4 5 6 7 8 9 10

This book is dedicated to the millions of faithful believers persecuted by the Chinese Communist Party since 1949.

CONTENTS

FOREWORD

EVIL, UNCHECKED, IS A PRELUDE to genocide.

As a novelist—the author of political thrillers about evil regimes and wicked ideologies and the worst-case scenarios that can unfold if good people are unaware or do nothing—what I write can be shocking to many readers.

I make no apologies. Sometimes we need to be shocked. Sometimes fiction is the best way to capture people's imagination and help them understand the truth. Sometimes a novel is the only way—or most effective way—to help people truly understand the real world threats facing them, get them to wake up, and mobilize them to take action before it is too late.

Still, ultimately, novels are works of fiction. The nightmare scenarios I paint for my readers about terror, war, and genocide, have not happened. Not yet. I pray they never will. But I'm not only trying to entertain; I'm trying to educate, warn, and catalyze people to action.

That's exactly what I'm doing in my most recent thriller, *The Beijing Betrayal*. Communist China hasn't invaded Taiwan—yet. The CCP hasn't attacked American and allied forces throughout the Pacific to neutralize US power and dominate the entire Pacific Rim—yet. Nor has Beijing unleashed mass casualty terror attacks inside the United States in close coordination with the Iranian regime and other radical Islamist forces—yet.

However, this is not the case with *China's War on Faith.* This isn't fiction. This stuff is real. Too real.

And terrifying.

I harbor no illusions that the Chinese Communist Party has been a paragon of virtue in this world. Far from it. The more I learn about the evil it has perpetrated in Tibet, in Xinjiang, against Christians—and what it's capable of doing and want to do against the free and democratic people of Taiwan—the more horrified and sickened I am.

Still, reading about the genocides the Communist Chinese leaders are committing, and planning, and the world is largely ignoring—and learning so much more about them thanks to the incredibly courageous testimonies of the survivors in this book—brought these atrocities to a whole new level for me.

Many have sounded the alarm in recent years, but I can't think of a more suitable messenger than my friend, Sam Brownback. I first met him in 1994 when he was elected to serve as a US Congressman. We have remained good friends through his service as a Senator, a Governor, and as the US Ambassador for International Religious Freedom. And along the way I have come to deeply respect his character, honesty, and commitment to discovering and communicating the truth, whatever the cost.

As a man of deep faith, and a former government official serving at the highest levels and all over the world, Sam comes to this book armed with plenty of facts and figures. And I've learned so much from him. But I've found that the real power of his message comes in the personal conversations he has had with the survivors of extreme persecution and with their horrific accounts of what China has been doing in the shadows.

I am so grateful to Sam for his role in drawing my attention to China. For most of my life, I have focused on and written about emerging and imminent threats to Israel and in the broader Arab/Muslim world. Indeed, I love and work in Jerusalem and travel extensively throughout North Africa and the Middle East. Yet, as an author and journalist—and as a devout Christian from a Jewish background—I have always sought to keep my fingers on the pulse of world affairs. Thus, I have made it a practice to travel to different trouble spots around the world. And over the last decade, my attention has been drawn more and more to China as experts like Sam, former Secretary of State Mike Pompeo, and others have helped me understand both the evil and the urgency.

My concerns about Beijing's cruel vision of global domination and eradication of religious faith have grown exponentially—and it should concern you, as well. The grave and growing threat posed by the CCP to global freedom and security is precisely why I wrote *The Beijing Betrayal.* It's also precisely why I immediately agreed to endorse and write the foreword to this powerful and timely book.

Let's be clear: Communist China coddles the worst of dictators and seeks them as allies. It bribes and bullies developing countries to make them pliant. It stands for everything that America and the West is against. It must be exposed. And stopped.

Indeed, if China is not stopped, and soon, the world will be a far darker and more dangerous place and I don't know if it would ever recover. The surveillance technology they sell to every dictator and despot makes these evil leaders even harder to remove from power—and far more effective in subjugating their own people.

I encourage you to not only read this book but to stand with the brave souls profiled here to stop this relentless attack on their most basic freedom and ours: The right to pray to—and serve wholeheartedly—the God we love and follow. A right, I'm sorry to say, we too often take for granted.

Let your blood boil with indignation. Then pray. And act. Now.

No country will be spared in China's battle for global supremacy. The Chinese Communist Party is an atheistic entity that pushes its allies to choke out all religions that don't bow to the State.

Time is short. No person of faith is safe.

It's certainly not the world I want to leave for my children and grandchildren.

How about you?

—Joel C. Rosenberg

INTRODUCTION

THREE GENOCIDES

THE CHINESE COMMUNIST PARTY (CCP) is waging a war on faith, a war that it could win if we don't wake up and start fighting. With everything we have.

And this is a war that China *must* lose.

Because what China is doing—what we are permitting China to do—brings back chilling memories of the Holocaust.

The campaign was fought for many years on the local level. Now it is coordinated at the very top of the Chinese government and with the kind of technology that should make all of us terrified.

Not just on a moral level. Because we care about the Chinese believers who are the victims of horrifying persecution today.

We should be terrified because China's war on faith can come here. To the United States. I can make the case that it already has.

The Chinese have taken the war to authoritarian countries like Iran and Nicaragua, where surveillance technology enables the persecution of Muslims who object to Islamist repression of women, and Catholic priests who offer a creed different from Marxism.

The CCP is also winning here, in free capitalist America, where two huge businesses, Hollywood and the National Basketball

Association, have become willing enforcers of Chinese censorship. Censorship that has shielded China's crimes against humanity—the internment of hundreds of thousands, forced abortion and sterilization, organ harvesting from living victims—from international notice and protest.

The movie industry is in bed with the Chinese because it often relies on the Asian market to make a profit.

The NBA's star players sell shoes in China. How hypocritical it was several years ago when these incredibly well-paid athletes never uttered a negative word about what was going on in China, while condemning our own society.

Only one player has called out the Chinese Communists—Enes Kanter Freedom, the third overall pick in the 2011 NBA Draft, whose story I tell in this book. He no longer plays in the league, and that's because he had the audacity to speak out against China's oppression. Yes, Black Lives Matter, but what about Chinese lives? Don't they matter, too?

Look, I'm as fervent a believer in the capitalist system as the next guy, siding with big business throughout my years as a congressman, senator, and governor. That does not mean, however, that we should be doing business with everyone.

Certainly not with a regime that is waging a war on religion and conducting genocide against the Uyghur Muslims in Xinjiang, the practitioners of Falun Gong, and the Buddhists in Tibet—and persecuting Christians who refuse to put the CCP above the Bible.

With their relentless pursuit of the almighty dollar and cheap products, a number of American businesses are acting as accomplices. In 2023, US companies' investment in China totaled $127 billion. That's billion with a *B*. Those companies include Apple, BlackRock, JPMorgan Chase, and Tesla. Here's a quote attributed to Vladimir Lenin. "We will hang the capitalists with the rope they sell us."

China has been waging this war—in one form or another, on one religion or another—for nearly eighty years, since 1949, when Mao Zedong defeated the Nationalist forces and Chiang Kai-shek fled to Taiwan. Today, the war is being fought more aggressively than ever, by a government led by a Mao-like dictator, Xi Jinping.

Let me share with you a few examples of what China has been doing:

- Pressuring Christians to replace pictures of Jesus with posters of Xi Jinping
- Arresting priests who do not acknowledge the Chinese Communist Party as the ultimate authority. Catholic bishops in China are in prison or have disappeared, or live under house arrest or surveillance
- Detaining Uyghurs, a mostly Muslim, Turkic-speaking ethnic group who live in the northwestern province of Xinjiang, in concentration camps—at least one with a crematorium attached, as Ethan Gutmann, a senior fellow at the Victims of Communism Memorial Foundation, reported to Congress in 2022
- Harvesting organs from prisoners who are still alive—both Uyghurs and practitioners of Falun Gong—to support the country's billion-dollar organ export industry
- Subjecting Uyghurs to pregnancy tests, forced intrauterine devices, and forced abortions
- Demolishing sacred religious sites. Chinese authorities destroyed five thousand mosques over a single three-

month period, and 97 percent of Tibetan Buddhist monasteries and nunneries are now gone

- Forcing teachers to give up Christian beliefs and practices

Historians and academics have written extensively about this subject in books, magazines, newspapers, and on the internet. But their facts and figures haven't led to the policy changes at the highest level of government, in America and abroad, that must be implemented to win the war.

And time is not on our side. Every day, innocent people in China are being imprisoned, tortured, raped. Killed.

I'm not a historian or an academic. I'm a former congressman, senator, and governor from Kansas who served as the US ambassador-at-large for international religious freedom during the first Trump administration. I've been privileged to work in the trenches with valiant fighters for freedom of religion who have been thorns in China's side for decades. And privileged to speak face-to-face with survivors—Christians and Muslims, practitioners of Falun Gong, Tibetan Buddhist monks—who have stayed true to their beliefs despite feeling the brunt of brutal Chinese persecution.

Their stories have moved me to tears. My hope is that sharing their experiences will inspire the policy changes that the experts' facts and statistics haven't been able to bring about. Stories are more powerful than data.

I will introduce you to some of the most inspiring people I have ever had the honor to meet. It's because of them that I have reason for hope, even in the darkest moments, of which there are far too many. These people of faith are similar to the Jewish *refuseniks* of the 1970s and '80s (so named because the Soviet Union refused their request to emigrate to Israel), incredibly brave souls such as Natan Sharansky, who spent nine years in a Siberian prison. While small in number, they challenged the legitimacy of the Russian Communist regime and helped crush the Soviet Union. Or, as President Ronald Reagan rightly put it, "the Evil Empire."

Some of these men and women have suffered for years behind bars, others enduring physical torture. They lost family members and friends and were subjected to unimaginable assaults on their privacy and their personal integrity. Every story demonstrates the cruelty of the regime that poses the greatest threat to freedom in our lifetime. Even greater than the Soviet Union during the Cold War, something I never thought was possible. But none of this horrific persecution deterred them from fighting for their right, and the rights of others, to practice their faith.

The war is being conducted by the CCP, not by the Chinese people themselves, whom I have admired since my first visit in 1985 (my wife, Mary, and I are blessed to have a brilliant daughter adopted from China) and led by Xi Jinping, the president of China since 2013 and general secretary of the Communist Party since 2012. In fact, the CCP has killed more of its own people than any regime in history—more than Adolf Hitler's Germany or Joseph Stalin's Russia. By far. Let that sink in for a little bit.

For the longest time, I could not understand how so much of the civilized world, armed with overwhelming evidence from eyewitnesses, could be silent while Hitler's Third Reich carried out the Final Solution against the Jews of Europe.

Now I understand. I understand too well.

Because it is happening again, before our very eyes—in the twenty-first century, no less, in a world where everyone has a smartphone, with access to the facts and the pictures at their fingertips. Facts and pictures from *three* genocides that China has perpetuated: Uyghurs with shaved heads loaded on trains to concentration camps, Tibetan Buddhist monks in chains, the face of a thirty-seven-year-old woman burned with electric batons for practicing Falun Gong. The consequences for freedom everywhere—and that includes the United States of America—will be dire if we fail to act. I pray that it is not already too late.

I can hear the skeptics now. *I'm worried about putting food on the table and keeping my kids safe in school. I feel horrible for the people who are suffering in China, but what does that have to do with me and my family?*

More than you can imagine.

China is intent on destroying Western civilization, replacing it with its own world order of Communism, Atheism, and Totalitarianism. Where nothing will matter, not even God, except Xi Jinping, the Chinese Communist Party, and the other dictators in its dangerous orbit.

Do you want to live in a world like that?

And if we were to lose the freedom of religion, guaranteed in the First Amendment to the Constitution and in the United Nations' Universal Declaration of Human Rights, what right would we lose next? Freedom of speech? Freedom of assembly? Our essential freedoms go together—and they can fall together. In a flash. History, if nothing else, has taught us that.

★ ★ ★

Consider the Uyghurs. The genocide against them is the front in the war on faith that is probably most known about in America. The Uyghurs live in East Turkistan, a region of China the CCP refers to as the Xinjiang Uyghur Autonomous Region. The Uyghurs, with close ties to the surrounding Central Asian nations, have enjoyed a glorious history with enchanting music, dance, and literature.

A history in danger of being eradicated. As if it never existed.

As Secretary of State Mike Pompeo said on the last day of the first Trump administration in January 2021, "We are witnessing the systematic attempt to destroy Uyghurs by the Chinese party-state."

The first phase, which began in August 2016, was organized by Chen Quanguo, the Communist Party boss in Xinjiang and China's version of the sadistic Nazi SS leader Heinrich Himmler. He had previously been in charge of the repression in Tibet.

Chen Quanguo recruited thousands of police officers to work in tandem with high-level security forces and set up cameras—at intersections, inside taxis and buses, you name it—every two to three hundred meters. With the enhanced surveillance, the CCP collected data to assemble profiles of individuals it deemed suspicious, many of whom would eventually be detained.

"The checkpoints made movement very hard," according to Adrian Zenz, a senior fellow and director of China studies at the Victims of Communism Memorial Foundation.

"People couldn't even go to the next village without permission. This was complemented by extremely intrusive visits at the village level, work teams going door-to-door, asking people, 'Do you eat pork? And if not, why not?' If people didn't eat pork, that would be one of the reasons they would be detained for reeducation."

Next was the second phase: the construction of internment camps, where the "reeducation" would take place.

Another reminder of the Holocaust.

It is estimated that the camps held up to as many as 1.8 million Uyghur prisoners in 2020, including women forced to undergo sterilization and abortions. Roughly eighty percent of the children in one Uyghur preschool, reportedly, had at least one parent in the camps.

The parent detained, Zenz told me, has usually been "the head of the household. You can imagine what that does for a family."

In families where both parents were taken away, children were sent to orphanages and brainwashed into believing the government had no other alternative to keep the country safe.

The authorities claimed the camps were "vocational and training centers."

Nonsense. They were designed to wipe out the Uyghur religion, culture, and identity, simple as that.

Victims of Communism fellow Ethan Gutmann told Congress about someone he interviewed who "said he drove by the crematorium every day and the smell was a common complaint among local workers."

When I read Gutmann's testimony, I thought of the ovens at Auschwitz. And every other image of the Final Solution.

A large percentage of the Uyghurs who were able to avoid the camps became, in a way, prisoners in their own homes, the Chinese placing informants to live with them to make sure they didn't practice their Muslim faith. The CCP, as I mentioned before, have also destroyed thousands of mosques and removed Islamic-style architecture and symbols from others.

There has been no end to its cruelty.

More recently, the campaign against the Uyghurs appears, at first glance, to have become more benign. Many of the internment camps have been closed or repurposed, and there are fewer police visible on the streets.

Unfortunately, appearances are deceptive.

Many in the camps were moved into prisons and detention centers and given long sentences. Others were shipped to factories to build electronics, home appliances, footwear, and so forth. "People who used to be part of a rural community and had a lot of spare time and were harder to control," Zenz explained to me, "are now working in factories and living and sleeping on the compound." Which have become, in essence, he added, "a one-stop environment for control and assimilation."

I asked Zenz if the less visible police presence might make the environment feel less threatening to the Uyghurs.

In a word, no.

"They know what is going on," he explained. "They know they can end up back in prison anytime."

Then he said something that blew me away: The oppression of the Uyghurs has been, from the outset, "an incredibly calculated strategy. The Nazis seem almost unsophisticated compared to this."

To tell the story of the Uyghurs, I will introduce you to Mihrigul Tursun. If she doesn't break your heart, I don't know what will.

Mihrigul, thirty-six, now resides in Arlington, Virginia, a Washington, DC, suburb. She went through hell before she fled China in the fall of 2018, and she is still going through hell. She lost a nursing child and most of the hearing in her right ear, and to this day she has nightmares in which she is taken away by the Chinese police. In addition, as with many others who have been fortunate enough to get out, she experiences transnational oppression from a regime that doesn't see any limits. The Chinese know where she is.

Yet despite it all, she is determined to get the truth out. No matter how many times she is forced to relive it.

I've met a lot of courageous people in my travels around the world. I've never met anyone more courageous than Mihrigul Tursun.

I have a great deal of admiration for two other brave women as well: Wang Chunyan and Frances Hui.

Chunyan, a follower of Falun Gong—a spiritual practice that, drawing on ancient Buddhist and Taoist traditions and teachings, blends meditation and exercise with a commitment to the tenets of truth, compassion, and tolerance—lost everything. Her business. Her home. Her husband.

Nonetheless, Chunyan, seventy years old, will continue, like Mihrigul, to speak out against what the CCP has done. The Chinese repression of Falun Gong is China's second genocide in progress.

The list of atrocities against Falun Gong practitioners, to repeat, includes harvesting organs while the donors are still alive. The Uyghurs have been victims of this grisly practice, as well.

Frances Hui, who grew up in Hong Kong and took an active role in the city's pro-democracy protests in 2019 and 2020, has also lost more than she ever could have anticipated. And she has yet to turn thirty.

Now living in Washington, DC, as the first Hong Kong activist to receive political asylum in the United States, Frances hasn't seen her parents for several years, and there is a bounty on her head.

She, too, won't stop telling the truth. Wherever it may lead.

Then there is Pastor Pan Yongguang, leader of the Mayflower Church—the name couldn't be more appropriate—whose sixty-four members escaped from China in 2019 to an island in South Korea. After a couple of years, they moved to Thailand and eventually ended up in, of all places, Midland, Texas. Where they are free to study and preach the Gospel without fear. I have spent a lot of time with the God-loving souls who embarked on this long, treacherous journey, and I still find their story hard to believe. Especially the part about the five-foot-three pregnant woman who stood up to the Thai police when her life and the lives of the other church members were in serious danger.

I will tell you the story of Arjia Rinpoche, a high-ranking Buddhist lama in Tibet who was only eight years old when his life changed forever. One day in 1958, soldiers from the People's Liberation Army showed up at his monastery. Many of the monks, deemed by the CCP to be counterrevolutionaries, were dragged out of the crowd to be humiliated. And tortured.

As Arija has written, one monk, bound with rope, "curled up under the blows, the sound of his pain coming from deep in his throat.... For three interminable hours, more and more people were bound, hauled to the platform, and denounced."[1] By day's end, the Chinese had arrested about five hundred monks. The story that Arjia, who escaped to America in the late 1990s, tells is of a religion and culture being strangled before our very eyes, the third ongoing genocide by the Chinese, another the world has chosen to ignore.

I will also introduce you to Enes Kanter Freedom, who played in the National Basketball Association for more than a decade. Until, despite numerous warnings from league officials, he continued to call out Xi Jinping's government for its mistreatment of the Uyghurs and Tibetans.

Enes didn't have to say a word. He was living his dream, and besides, he's not Chinese. He's Turkish. Yet he felt an obligation to stand up for what is right, whatever the consequences, and he has no regrets.

If only more athletes would display such courage. It could make a huge difference.

Meanwhile, in profiling Frank Wolf (I don't like to think where the struggle for religious freedom would be without him) and Nina Shea, a senior fellow at the Hudson Institute, a think tank in Washington, DC, I will show why courage is also required in the framing of public policy.

Frank made a secret—and risky—trip to Tibet in 1997. I still don't know how he pulled it off.

Nina is deeply committed to her Catholic faith. She is also deeply committed to exposing wrongdoing. I pray that the facts she revealed in 2024 on the ten bishops incarcerated in China, some of whom are in their nineties, make you as angry as they make me.

I cannot end this introduction without mentioning two remarkable individuals who have played a huge role in China's Christian community.

The first is eighty-five-year-old Peter Xu, one of the fathers of the "house church" movement. Peter was imprisoned on five occasions from the mid-1960s through late 1990s and was constantly on the run.

The second is Wang Yi, a Protestant pastor who has been in a Chinese prison since December 2018. Wang, a prominent human rights lawyer before he found his calling as a pastor, is the only person I profiled whom I was unable to interview. I met him two decades ago while I was in the Senate, but I haven't talked to him since. Through his acts of defiance, his powerful sermons and the recollections of those who know him well, it is easy to understand why he is seen as such a heroic figure in China and abroad.

And as such a dangerous figure by the Chinese government.

"Separate me from my wife and children, ruin my reputation, destroy my life and my family, the authorities are capable of doing all of these things," he said in a letter he wrote before the arrest he knew was coming. "However, no one in this world can force me to renounce my faith."

★ ★ ★

Why is China waging this war? A war against its own people.

Because religion poses the most serious threat to the CCP's dictatorship. It has a powerful moral authority of its own, independent of the Chinese dictatorship. Xi Jinping and the other Communist leaders know that. Just as Mao and his successors knew it. To control man, Communist tyrants know they have to control faith and reliance on a higher being, a source of standards beyond this world. Karl Marx hated religion from the beginning. His followers have felt the same way.

In the Soviet Union, the objective was to create the "New Soviet man"—a cog in a crushing, grinding machine. With a mind for reason but no soul for God.

The goals of the Chinese are no different.

And like the Russians during the Cold War, they have reason to be fearful. People of faith will risk everything for what they believe in.

Consider what led to the fall of the Evil Empire in 1991.

Without Ronald Reagan and British Prime Minister Margaret Thatcher, the Soviet Union would not have broken up and the Berlin Wall would not have come down. But John Paul II was the third indispensable figure. "Be not afraid," the pope said in a 1979 outdoor Mass attended by millions in Warsaw that inspired the Polish people into action and led to the government's collapse a decade later.

Which is why it is essential that Pope Leo XIV call out China for its numerous atrocities.

As I indicated earlier, its war on faith goes back a long way.

Tibet fell victim in the 1950s, Chinese troops eventually marching into Lhasa, the capital and one of the most spiritual cities in the world. Tens of thousands of Tibetans were killed, and the Dalai Lama, their spiritual leader, fled into exile in India, where he remains today. He is now ninety years old.

During Mao's Cultural Revolution, which began in 1966 and lasted a decade, the war on faith entered a new, more dangerous phase. Religious activities were banned, bishops arrested, temples and shrines destroyed.

Fast-forward to Xi Jinping.

In 2016, Xi called for the "Sinicization" of religion in China. Five years later, he stated that the country must "insist on uniting the masses of religious believers around the party and the government."

For years, as I mentioned before, the war was waged on a regional level, with some provinces more tolerant of religion than others. Not anymore. The agencies responsible are now under the control of the central authorities. And what makes the situation more alarming than ever is a weapon that the Chinese didn't possess in the past to the degree they do now:

Technology.

In other words, George Orwell's Big Brother (from his famous novel, *1984*) is alive and well, operating out of Beijing.

The technology—GPS sensors in smartphones and cars and the use of facial recognition, for starters—allows government officials to regulate the way millions of people practice their faith in public.

And, even more frightening, in private.

Download a picture of a religious leader or read a sacred spiritual text, the government may find out.

Same with meeting a friend at an underground house church.

Can you imagine living that way?

Wait until they get their currency fully digitized—and they're not far from it—so that they can track every financial transaction. They will be able to stop the flow of money to any person who defies the system. Already, the operators of the all-in-one apps for mobile phones that people in China rely on to pay for goods and services and communicate with friends have developed their own "content moderation" teams, in effect doing the censoring for the government, so that they won't be assessed a heavy fine or, worse yet, forced offline.

As for turning them off, that might not work, either.

Good luck trying to get around without a cell phone. You need one in most areas of the country to pay your bills, use public transportation, receive medical care, and so forth. Surveillance software with names like SkyNet, Police Cloud, and Sharp Eyes tracks a ton of activity. Everyone becomes afraid to take even the slightest risk.

This is the present day for Chinese believers. But it could easily be our future, as well. China has already exported its surveillance technology to more than eighty countries, so that those governments can wage their own war on faith. Fifty nations have bought AI Safe City or Smart City surveillance technologies from a Chinese company, Huawei, including Algeria, Armenia, Bangladesh, Botswana, Chile, Ecuador, Egypt, France (!), Ghana, Indonesia...and on down the alphabet.

Iran, for example, purchased a surveillance system from Tiandy, another Chinese company, that enables officials to better monitor landline and mobile communications. Another example is Nicaragua, led once again by Daniel Ortega, the Marxist revolutionary. In 2023, the chief of Nicaragua's national police signed an agreement to cooperate on security with China's Ministry of State Security. That was at a "global security forum" where China showed off sinister new technologies for facial recognition, surveillance cameras, and DNA matching. The Chinese are training thousands of security agents from other countries every year, and the number is growing.

To adopt a sports analogy, the CCP is building a strong bench of nations who are dependent on its technology.

And on China.

Even so, I remain hopeful that the war can be won.

Despite its immense power, the Chinese regime is, at its core, weak. It could crumble at any moment, having no legitimacy with the people, which is why it constantly worries about what's going on in *the street.* If China were to lose the street, there would be no release valve. The release valve would be the leaders of the CCP forced into exile.

China is weak, in no small part, because of how it has dealt with God, with the yearning inside all of us for the transcendent. We ask ourselves the same questions that have haunted man since the dawn of time and that will never go away: What comes after this? Did the world come together by chance, or is there a design? If there is a design, is there a designer?

Most people find the answers to these questions in religion, and when they do, they cling to it. The Chinese have long been a very spiritual people. But the CCP is constantly forcing its citizens to abandon that search for meaning and punishing them if they resist.

It boils down to a fight between the Kingdom of Man and the Kingdom of God. The Kingdom of Man may take the early rounds, which can last for decades, even centuries. But in the end, the Kingdom of God will win out. We didn't know it at the time, but when Pope John Paul II told the people, "Be not afraid," Communism in Poland was already as good as dead. And before long, throughout the Soviet bloc.

I have a small piece of the Berlin Wall at my home in Kansas. It reminds me of the eventual fate of all things evil.

Which one day, I have no doubt, will include the Chinese Communist Party.

The only question: How long it will take and how many more innocent people will go to prison or die?

In every period of history, God presents us with moral tests.

How we confront China's war on faith is one of ours. As I was once told by a former leader of the Tibetan government in exile, "Either the world will change China, or China will change the world."

Part One

THE WAR ON CHRISTIANS

CHAPTER 1

THE BILLY GRAHAM OF CHINA

PETER XU NEVER LOST FAITH in his Lord and Savior.

Not even when death was near. Especially when death was near.

In 1997, Peter hung from the metal bars of a sliding prison door for nearly four hours. At one point, the guards—cogs in the system, I keep reminding myself—opened the door as wide as they could, stretching his chest so far out that he could barely breathe. The pain was excruciating, and it would only get worse.

Peter was not a young man. He was in his late fifties, one of the fathers of the house church movement in China.

Why was God allowing him to be tortured? None of the servants in His kingdom were more obedient than Peter Xu, more loving. Often at great risk to himself and his family.

Peter knew why.

"I saw it as my portion of the sufferings of Christ," Peter, now living in Colorado, told me. "I could feel the imprint of the Cross on me like I was being seared with the Cross. It made me love Jesus even more."

Peter, who often quotes verses from the New Testament, proceeded to quote Revelation 1:9. "I, John, your brother and companion in the suffering and kingdom and patient endurance that are ours in Jesus...."[2]

This was the fifth time Peter had been sent to prison.

His crime?

Spreading the Gospel of Jesus Christ.

★ ★ ★

Peter Xu was born on October 6, 1940, in Zhenping County, in the province of Henan, during the middle of the Japanese occupation of China (1937–1945), one of the most brutal occupations in history. Its horrors are less known because it has been overshadowed, then and since, by the Nazi atrocities in Europe.

Peter's first house church got started for reasons that had nothing to do with Communist persecution. In fact, his family had a church in their house even before Mao and the Communist Party ruled China. As a child, Peter's grandmother had her feet tightly bound to preserve what was considered a sign of beauty in those days: tiny feet. But for the rest of her life, the pain and deformity caused by the foot binding limited how far she could walk. Peter's family resided in a rural area far from the closest church. So his parents started a church in their home.

That was the way their branch of the house church movement got going.

The idea caught on. After the Communists took over, the "Born Again Movement" of house churches that Peter led was a literal Godsend.

His grandmother's deformed feet had been a blessing from God. To paraphrase Genesis: *What man meant for evil, God meant for good.*[3]

In the 1960s, when Christian churches were outlawed altogether in the Cultural Revolution, house churches were the only places Christians could worship. And then after the Cultural

Revolution, when churches were allowed to reopen but required to adhere to the Three-Self Patriotic Movement—the organization the Chinese had founded in 1954 to make Protestant churches subject to the Communist Party—the unregistered house churches became a vehicle for Christians who insisted on putting God above government to keep up their faith and their fellowship. Peter's Born Again Movement became one of the main house church branches in China, eventually attracting an estimated twenty million members.

When Peter was five, he had a vision, a revelation of the Trinity that has been a source of inspiration ever since, through imprisonment, torture, hunger, and a life on the run in hiding from the authorities.

What he saw is that all life is from God, and ultimately we must give Him an account of what we do with the life He gave us.

Peter's vision came just a few years before Mao and the Communists seized power and everything turned upside down.

Before that, Christians and Christianity were welcome in China—embraced actually, with missionaries from all corners of the globe spreading the Gospel. No longer. The Communists are atheists who see Christianity as a tool of Western imperialism. By 1958, the churches across the Chinese countryside had been shut down; only a handful of urban churches remained open, and they were for foreigners.

When Peter was twenty-four, he worked in a coal-mining facility with about seven thousand others.

It wasn't his choice. The government had sent him there, hundreds of miles from his home, after he had lost his previous job.

One day, the leadership at the facility was instructed by the authorities to select one percent of the workforce for an extra level of ideological cleansing as part of the Four Cleanups Movement, a campaign by the Chinese to rid the party of corruption at the rural level. The cleansing would pave the way for the Cultural Revolution a couple of years later. Peter was one of seventy workers on the list turned over to the Communist authorities.

The seventy were publicly criticized and humiliated—and tortured. So badly that some escaped the only way they could. By committing suicide.

Peter told me about one man who, on the way to a cleansing session, grabbed a nail and half of a brick and killed himself by driving the nail into his ear canal. Another man threw himself into a large iron wok for boiling water and died from the burns. Others went insane. The Chinese literally bullied people to death.

But Peter had a comfort and a strength that his fellow workers didn't have. That led him not to give up. That told him it was a time for love, for trust. In the Lord.

For him, suicide was never an option.

"I would not have been able to see the face of God," he explained. "As a Christian, we don't have a right to take our own life."

So, all the time he was subjected to the humiliation and the torture, he kept praying. He reminded himself of a hymn his grandmother had taught him when he was a boy. He sang the hymn for me during one of our interviews: "Trust and obey, for there's no other way to be happy in Jesus, but to trust and obey."

Although he had survived the cleansing, Peter's troubles were far from over. He got married, and he and his wife, Liu Shifang, started a family, but the Chinese would not leave them alone. They'd had spies in Peter's church since 1960, Communists pretending to be Christian worshippers. The family took off for Peter's parents' house in Hubei Province. But Peter was deemed a "counterrevolutionary," and he and Liu weren't safe there, either.

The party made sure Liu didn't find any work. Worse yet, she was forced to divorce Peter.

I asked Peter where he called home in those days. He told me he had no home. Until the spring of 2001, when he was free to leave for the United States.

For years, the police harassed his family, demanding that they reveal where Peter was hiding.

They didn't say a word, until finally, in September 1969, they broke down and revealed where he was. Government forces surrounded the location, but fortunately Peter was gone by the time the soldiers arrived.

Being a fugitive in his own country didn't stop Peter from preaching the Gospel. Nothing could.

He found fellow Christian believers who took him into their homes for weeks, even months. He prayed with them and held Bible study classes, often in the dark. This went on year after year as a network of worshippers grew slowly, steadily, across the land.

Peter taught repentance first, then salvation.

"The key to revival," he said, "was back to Jesus and His Cross."

In 1982, Peter finally was caught, arrested, and sent to a labor camp. Amazingly, he managed to escape. The ordeal, however, didn't slow him down; he went right back to evangelizing for his Lord and Savior. In 1985, he launched his first Christian seminary to train pastors and lay people. And seven more "house seminaries" the next year. Peter was well prepared for this step. He had been putting together a curriculum in his mind for decades. Now that things in China were opening up after the Cultural Revolution (the people, he told me, were tired of the evils of Communism and were seeking the spiritual value of life), here was the opportunity he had been longing for. Praying for. Believers showed up at night to avoid the authorities, and stayed.

For a week, a month, even six months. Some dug holes under these houses where they could study and worship and survive. They didn't dare to leave.

The seminaries weren't sanctioned by the government, but they weren't shut down, either.

Even so, one could not be too careful. "Opening up," in China, has long been a relative term. As some observers in the United States suspected, the Chinese were biding their time, waiting for the moment to continue the class struggle and the drive for global Communism.

In the spring of 1988, Peter was told that Billy Graham, who was making his first visit to China, the native land of his wife Ruth—her parents had been missionaries—wanted to meet with him.

Peter, who was often referred to as the Billy Graham of China, couldn't have been more excited.

The Reverend Graham was the best-known evangelical Christian leader in America—and around the world. Since the late 1940s, he had been delivering sermons to packed stadiums and arenas everywhere, many shown on TV, and had strong relationships with Presidents Eisenhower, Johnson, and Nixon. Billy Graham was the closest thing we've had in modern times to a person who spoke for Protestant Christians worldwide.

He had heard of the work Peter was doing and wanted to learn more. What was happening to the Chinese Church was a matter of great interest to the global Christian community, and it was also a great mystery—particularly since all the foreign missionaries had been kicked out.

The Communists had their own reasons for inviting the Reverend Graham to China.

The CCP wanted to promote its own church—the Three-Self Patriotic Movement, which, with its socialist propaganda, was more government than church. What better way to authenticate this government-led church than by having the one-and-only Billy Graham preach in it? (Peter was never fooled by the Three-Self Patriotic Movement. He saw it for what it is: an attempt to neutralize the legitimate church as a prelude to eliminating it once and for all.)

For the meeting to take place, everything needed to be arranged in secret. The Chinese never would have allowed Peter to visit with a religious figure so prominent on the world scene. It would give Peter way too much standing in China. Billy Graham, for his part, couldn't demand such a meeting, or the whole trip might have been canceled and he would have lost the opportunity to preach to the Chinese people.

On the morning of the day that he and the Reverend Graham were set to have their secret meeting, Peter was waiting in a park for his final instructions when a stranger tapped him on the shoulder.

"Let's go for a walk," the stranger said.

Peter was led to a police station that was packed with members of the Three-Self Church. They took him to a run-down garden where, on the other side of a wall, there was a registration office for a Beijing prison. He was put in room No. 14. (Why that particular detail stands out in his memory, I have no idea.)

Once he was alone, he prayed.

"God," he said, "it wasn't me who wanted to see Billy Graham. He reached out and wanted to see me. I was praying for this, but there was never a sign of an obstacle from you."

Peter wondered, *Will this, after everything I've been through, be the end for me?*

He was allowed two meals a day. He ate only one. Every other day, he fasted completely. Peter planned to keep it up until God took him to Heaven. Which he felt sure would happen any moment.

After three years, however, the Chinese let him go.

He went back to his life's mission: Spreading the Gospel.

In 1991, at a house church theology teachers' retreat, he met Guan Qingjing (her English name is Ruth). In 1996, they got married.

Three months later, Peter was arrested again—along with Ruth and half a dozen other members of his underground church.

Which bring us back to those four hours on His Cross.

"I felt Jesus' sadness for our sins," he said, "but how happy He was to take them on."

After about three hours, a guard came up from behind him: "Just surrender and it will be over."

I didn't ask Peter why he didn't give the guards what they wanted.

I knew the answer. I knew he would prefer to die than to abandon Jesus.

At first, Peter couldn't understand why the guards hated him so much. What had he ever done to them? Then it hit him. They hated him because they didn't know the God he served. They didn't know because no one had told them about Him.

"God," Peter said, certain he was down to his final breaths, "if you let me out of here, I will preach the Gospel to everyone I can from now on."

Either way, he couldn't lose.

When it's over, he thought, *I will be received by God. If we suffer for God, we are a sacrifice unto God.*

Just then, a guard released him from the metal bars.

The warden showed up with a paper and pen. Expecting that Peter, who was barely alive, would finally confess that God was a hoax.

"What do you have to say for yourself?" the warden asked.

"Thank you for allowing me to suffer for Christ," Peter said.

The warden was beside himself. "He's a real Christian," he told the guards.

★ ★ ★

By 2000, the Chinese were lobbying heavily for Most Favored Nation status, and Bill Clinton, with only months remaining in his presidency, was ready to give it to them. The United States–China Relations Act of 2000 passed the Congress in September of that year, a big step toward granting the country permanent normal trade relations with the US.

I was one of eighty-three senators who voted yes, and I have regretted it ever since.

Although my conscience has been eased somewhat by the fact that the vote may have led to Peter getting out of prison. And quite possibly, saved his life—he was in his sixties at the time. (From what I've been able to gather, President Clinton had made it clear that if Peter were allowed to emigrate to the United States, we would help him.)

Years later, when I was governor, I had my first extended conversation with Peter. He wanted to discuss my interest in Central Asia and share his own.

The first bill I sponsored in the Senate that became law was The Silk Road Strategy Act, a policy initiative to help the Central Asian countries that had broken away from the Soviet Union.

Along with many colleagues who tracked foreign policy, I was concerned that the countries could be drawn back into becoming client states for Russia or taken over by Muslim jihadist forces, creating more Afghanistans.

The law would encourage and facilitate them to bind together in commerce, transportation, and geopolitics along the ancient Silk Road trade route that linked East to West. I also saw it as an opportunity to build relationships in the region to advance religious freedom. Which would prove prescient when, serving in the first Trump administration two decades later, I helped get people of faith out of prison and worked on opening up religious institutions in that region.

Peter was interested in the Silk Road route, too. For an entirely different reason.

To carry the Gospel back to Jerusalem, finishing the circumnavigation that had started two thousand years before. Once again, he was living up to the promise he had made to God when he was hanging from the metal bars.

The Back to Jerusalem movement began in the 1920s when Chinese Christians received the Divine Call to carry the message of Jesus from China to Jerusalem. Christianity started in the Middle East, of course, spreading west to Rome, then to present-day France and Germany and the rest of continental Europe. Then on to England, the United States, South America, Asia… working its way back to Jerusalem.

At that first meeting, Peter asked what had given me the idea for the Silk Road bill.

I told him about when I was in Jerusalem, before heading to Central Asia for the first time. I was asleep in my hotel room when I was awakened by the words "Silk Road Strategy Act." They hit my mind like a brick.

I woke up, wrote everything down, then pondered and prayed: *What does this mean?*

Peter understood. I knew he would.

He seemed so peaceful and joyous for a man who had gone through what he had. And yet somehow I felt like we were both different threads in the same tapestry—"little pencils in God's Hand," as Mother Teresa would put it—seeking freedom for everyone in China, and around the world, to follow the convictions of their heart wherever that might lead them.

In one of my meetings with Peter, the interpreter translated what he was saying as "we must go through the mouth of the lion" to achieve what God calls us to do. Later Peter said that "we must *close* the mouth of the lion," referring to the dark spiritual forces behind Communism that must be stopped.

Peter, Ruth, his sister, Deborah, and countless other Chinese Christians are doing both. Their faith is incredible and infectious.

They are part of the work God is doing to end this night of wrong.

★ ★ ★

Peter Xu's amazing life story sums up the struggle for religious freedom that has been going on in the People's Republic of China since the Communists seized power in 1949—the ebbs and flows, from draconian persecution to temporary "openings up" and fragile "reforms." Outside observers—and perhaps the Chinese government itself—can never be certain when one period will end and another begin. But Peter, the quintessential man of faith, has been constant. He has spread the Gospel in season and out—no matter who was in charge in Beijing, what the official policy was, and what horrors were perpetrated upon him.

The CCP has tried to wipe out religion by forbidding it outright. That hasn't worked.

It created its own churches, trying to put the government over the Gospel. That hasn't worked, either.

The truth is, there is nothing the Chinese authorities can do to eliminate people's faith, regardless of how powerful the Communists think they are. The Kingdom of Man is limited. The Kingdom of God has no limits.

There is, on the other hand, a great deal that we can do.

We can support, forcefully and unapologetically, every individual's right to practice his or her faith. I can't repeat that often enough.

As comfortable as Peter seems to be in America, I have sensed that it can never be his home. And yet he cannot go back to his native country without taking terrible risks—of imprisonment, torture, even death. In our last interview, I asked him, "Do you yearn to go back to China?"

"As a servant called by the Lord," he answered, "I have no desire outside of Him. If He commands me, I will listen. If He sends me, I will go."

CHAPTER 2

A FARM BOY'S FAITH

I WAS THIRTEEN YEARS OLD when my life changed. Forever. Though I didn't realize it at the time.

I was riding a dirt bike in the field near our house outside Parker, Kansas, (population 250), taking a bucket of feed to the pigs in the back lot, one of my daily chores. We had about 600 pigs in different lots and pens, along with roughly 100 head of cattle and close to 1,000 laying hens. The work wasn't easy. I woke up around six o'clock with my siblings every weekday morning and was at it for nearly an hour, sometimes longer, before leaving for school. I don't recall ever having a choice.

My father was a farmer, as was his father before him and his father before that. Brownbacks, come to think of it, have been farmers in Kansas since just after the Civil War. (Once, speaking at a local banquet, I asked, "How many of you are a Brownback or related to a Brownback or think you're related to a Brownback?" Of the 250 or so people in the audience, roughly a third raised their hands.)

Dad started out with very little, living in a home without indoor plumbing, and died with more than a thousand acres of farmland that he and Mom had mostly purchased on their own.

Practically every dollar they earned went back into the farm, to buy more land and equipment or to cope with the ups and downs of the weather and the commodity markets. Each day, at precisely 12:21 p.m., the whole family sat at the dinner table in silence, listening to the farm report on the radio which detailed the latest prices. The prices of wheat, soybeans, corn, cattle, and hogs had an especially big impact on us and our livelihood. Dad needed to decide exactly when to sell which crops and ship the livestock to market to obtain the highest profits. He never actually thought he sold them at the right time, but he kept trying.

The broadcaster always gave the reasons for the fluctuation in prices: rains in Brazil, purchases by the Soviet Union, the most recent crop reports by the US Department of Agriculture, and so forth. Those were important moments around the dinner table.

We rarely went out for dinner, and when we did, we would have a burger and an ice cream cone, nothing fancy or expensive. Any steaks we ate were at home, from the cattle we had butchered for ourselves.

Mom and Dad worked long hours and didn't leave the farm overnight except when we went on our yearly family vacation—often in another part of the country—or when one of them was in the hospital: Mom to give birth, Dad for a broken back from a farming accident and, later, for colon cancer.

I always figured I would be a farmer, as well. I was looking forward to it, to be honest. While there were definitely times I resented the chores—my buddies would be off playing while I was toiling away—I learned the value of hard work, a lesson I have carried with me to this day. Once, after putting up bales of hay for hours and hours on a hot summer afternoon, Dad said to me, "So, you still think you want to farm?"

Absolutely.

I loved the outdoors, the smell of freshly tilled soil, mowed hay, or a spring shower, and the fact that we, as a family, were in it together, sink or swim.

Anyway, on the day my life changed, I was taking feed to the pigs when I suddenly brought my dirt bike to a halt. I put the bucket down, got down on my knees in the field, and confessed my sinfulness and desire to follow Jesus. I felt the call deep within my soul and responded.

Why then? Why there?

Because God, it occurred to me much later, loves humble places—Jesus, remember, was from Nazareth, which wasn't exactly a booming metropolis. And the back lot of a farm near Parker, Kansas, was about as humble a place as you could find. People in Parker didn't have a lot of income...well, except perhaps for Merlin Funk, who drove around town in a Cadillac. Still, we didn't think of ourselves as being poor; we just didn't have a lot of money. There's a big difference.

We were blessed. Blessed to live and work and worship the Lord in a community where everyone watched out for everyone else. If you ever got in trouble, the word spread so fast that your folks would know about it before you got home. I found my share—fighting with my two brothers and engaging in the familiar pranks at school—and when I did, the punishment was more manual labor. Dad figured if I had enough energy to fight, I had enough energy to work. He raised crops, but he was also raising men.

There weren't any police officers in Parker. We didn't seem to need any.

Wait, let me amend that.

There was a fella by the name of Pokey Smith, who was sort of a police officer, although no one ever saw him arrest anyone. Word was that he had acquired his badge by directing traffic at the county fair one year and deputized himself to be the so-called law in Parker. Pokey, who served in World War I, was probably about sixty-five but looked a hundred, and the old Chevy Bel Air he drove around town never went more than fifteen miles per hour. Besides, I don't believe the bib overalls he wore intimidated anyone.

The only real problems in Parker were the usual: drinking (a few friends died in car wrecks) and getting girls pregnant. By the night of my high school graduation in 1974, a friend and I figured that more than 40 percent of the girls we had started eighth grade with had gotten pregnant, engaged or married; mostly it was pregnancies. Fortunately, my faith kept me away from a number of problems that my peers experienced. Not all of them, but God's grace was surely at work—and I needed it.

My relationship with God didn't start the day I got on my knees in the back lot. He was important to me long before then.

So what took my faith to a whole other level? What made me surrender my life to Jesus?

It was the "Hounds of Heaven" and two youth group leaders who knew Jesus and loved the Lord. Their faith was real, joyful, infectious. *I want to be like that,* I thought.

In addition, my best friend's mother played the piano at the Methodist church I went to (one of two churches in Parker), which exposed me to more people of faith. That all this took place despite the fact that we didn't talk about spiritual matters in our house or say a prayer before meals, and that my parents rarely went to church—they would drop us kids off at Sunday school, Dad rushing back to work—could mean only one thing: The Lord was pursuing me. Not the other way around.

A significant influence on my soul was my great-grandmother Camilla Johnson. She was the sweetest woman in the world, different from everyone else. There was a peace about her that was palpable.

I believe she prayed for me, although she never mentioned it. My youth group leaders prayed for me. That I knew for sure.

The strangest thing was, I didn't feel any different from the moment I accepted Jesus. I took the feed to the pigs and went on with my day. The farm can't possibly survive unless everyone does their part. Only as the years went on did I grasp the significance of that morning in the field. By accepting Jesus as my Savior, I was embarking on a whole new journey. It began with being saved and decades later would include being sanctified.

I didn't tell my parents about what happened.

I didn't have to tell them. They saw me reading the Bible regularly and listening to Christian broadcasts on the radio while I shot baskets in our gravel driveway. I was still a teenager, my hormones going through the roof, but something different was going on with me, and they knew it.

★ ★ ★

Growing up, I didn't think I would go to college. What would be the point? From high school to the farm, that was the path I had planned.

Until I was awarded a National Honor Society scholarship when I was a senior in high school. The prize was $1,000, enough to cover tuition and books my freshman year at Kansas State University. The tuition, if I'm not mistaken, was $250 per semester. It would have been a waste not to go.

College was very good for the development of my mind. Even better for the development of my soul.

Scott Kalivoda, who lived directly across from me in the Marlatt Hall dormitory, led a Bible study group. He, like my great-grandmother, was different from everyone else. Everyone else wanted to party.

Despite being just a year older, Scott was a house parent to me in many ways. Fresh off the farm, I was exposed to one temptation after another. That's a lot for an eighteen-year-old to handle. I felt as if I were in a candy store and no one was behind the counter to tell me what I could or could not have. Except I didn't want to let Scott down. If I were to party with the others, surely he would find out, and I didn't want to feel the shame when I ran into him the next day. Scott showed me you can live a life of faith as a young man in college. Before I got to know him, I wasn't sure it was possible.

I didn't think about it at the time but later on, it occurred to me. *Why did Scott, of all people, happen to be the one who was living across the hall? What if it had been someone else? Would I have partied with the others instead of pursuing a deeper commitment to Jesus? If so, who knows where that path would have led me.*

It was no accident that it happened to be Scott. The Lord, to repeat, was pursuing me.

In college, thanks to Scott's encouragement, I joined the Navigators, a group focused on studying the Bible in a structured manner. Every morning, I had prayer time and read the Bible, getting myself ready for the day.

To follow the Lord, to serve the Lord.

I wasn't always successful, especially in the early days. Even in prayer, my mind would be occupied with a ton of different thoughts: this relationship or that class or whatever task I needed to get done. Thank goodness, with the help of some of the older men in the group who had been down the same route, I learned to understand that having distractions, and doubts, as well, was part of the journey—it still is—as I memorized the Words of Scripture. I knew I was on the right track.

My spiritual time then was ten to fifteen minutes in the morning. Now, I try to do ninety minutes throughout the day which often includes a half-hour mass. The higher God calls you, the more time you must spend in prayer and knowing Him and His ways.

Life gets in the way, of course. I don't always get a full hour and a half in. But when I don't, I miss it dearly. For the rest of that day, I'm more worldly and less spiritual than usual. And less at peace. We prepare our bodies every morning by showering, shaving, and brushing our teeth. Well, by having prayer time, I'm preparing my soul. If you ask me, preparing your soul is a lot more important than preparing your body.

For my prayer time, I try to get into a humble position, whether it's kneeling or sitting on the floor, and normally start with Psalm 100, a Psalm of praise and worship. "Shout joyfully to the Lord, all the earth," it says. "Serve the Lord with gladness and delight."[4]

This gets my mind in the right place.

From there, I move on to whatever may be on my heart on that given day. Much guidance, instruction, and peace come to me during this time of prayer.

One such time was at Kansas State when I was giving serious thought to running for student body president. In high school I had served as the state president of the Future Farmers of America (FFA), which showed me there was a big world outside Parker, Kansas, where I could do a lot of good. It was invigorating to lead others in a common cause. I wanted to do it again. My friends in the Navigators, on the other hand, thought it would be a mistake. They told me I should be more involved in Christian ministry work. That was where my soul would be enriched. Not in the messy world of student politics.

I prayed on it and had a real sense of peace and a calling to run for student body president. It occurred to me that there are many ways to serve the Lord and enrich your soul. I was chosen and derived a lot of satisfaction from aiding my fellow students.

After graduation, I headed back to Parker.

"Dad, I'm done with school," I said. "I'd like to talk to you about coming back to work on the farm."

He didn't hesitate for one second. "There's not room here for you."

I was taken aback.

"Don't you want to talk about it for a while? This is a very important decision."

Nope. End of conversation. End of being another Brownback to work the land.

It was a generous gift he gave me. A lot of farmers in those days encouraged their sons to join them. Don't get me wrong, I would have embraced the opportunity to continue in the long family tradition; my younger brother was already working with Dad. At K-State I was a farm broadcaster at the university's radio station and graduated with a degree in agriculture economics. I loved everything about this noble profession.

Only Dad knew what was better for me.

If I had joined the farm, it would in all likelihood have turned out very badly. This was shortly before the farm crisis of the early 1980s. I would have borrowed a lot of money to get started and ended up in bankruptcy, maybe taking Dad and the farm with me.

My calling was in public service and politics.

As the state president of the FFA, I attended a conference in Washington. That was a big deal back then, as folks from Parker rarely went on trips that far away. When I got home, I gave a slide show at the Methodist Church, showing everyone the White

House, the Capitol, and other historic sites. Better yet, I met the congressman from our district, Joe Skubitz, who had been in office since 1963. He was a jolly, kind man.

Congressman Skubitz was doing something important, serving his fellow citizens. All I could think of was, *How do I get a job like that?*

★ ★ ★

Upon graduating from Kansas State, I went to law school at the University of Kansas.

Which was where I met my future wife, Mary Margaret Stauffer. A city girl from Topeka, she was beautiful and smarter than me and more disciplined. I felt deep in my soul that here was someone I could walk through life with, and the fact that she, too, is a follower of Jesus has made us closer as the years have passed.

After law school, I joined a small firm in Manhattan—Manhattan, Kansas, that is—where I did everything: litigation, criminal law, contracts, wills, trusts, probate, family law, agricultural law, you name it. I represented a hospital, a bank, businesses, and two small cities, which gave me a glimpse into worlds I would later encounter as a policymaker, particularly involving government services for the less fortunate. (As a United States senator, I worked on prison reform, spending nights in jails and homeless shelters to understand the experience and environment. Though there was a huge difference between the others and myself: I would get out the next day. They would not.)

I focused on agricultural law as well, teaching at K-State and co-authoring two books on the subject.

Which led to applying to become the state's next secretary of agriculture. I wasn't too confident of landing the job—I didn't even tell the partners at the firm I was going for it—but I was selected as the state's youngest agriculture secretary ever.

My public life was off and running.

It was a challenging job, to say the least. The farm crisis was fully upon us, and the heartbreak it caused was difficult to watch. Many in Kansas lost their farms to bankruptcy and foreclosure, some committing suicide. Nearly one hundred banks closed or were forced to sell to another bank by regulators. The value of farmland fell to half of what it had been before. We tried everything we could to turn the situation around—alternative crops, biofuels, new technologies, and so forth. Sadly, there was only so much we could do.

After a couple of years, I thought about running for governor. Yes, I was only in my mid-thirties, but back then, I was always in a hurry.

As God would have it, my congressman, Jim Slattery, who had served for a decade, called me in 1993 with a message I will never forget: "I just want to let you know that I'm going to run for governor of Kansas. This has probably never happened before in Kansas history that a Democrat has told a Republican what their plays are before it has been made public, but I wanted you to know."

Those were different days, indeed.

My timing—or rather, God's timing—couldn't have been better. The 1994 election was known as the Republican Revolution, with the Grand Old Party picking up fifty-four seats, and, for the first time since 1952, seizing the majority in the House of Representatives. Even Tom Foley lost, the first sitting Speaker to be toppled since the Civil War. I prevailed in my race with 65 percent of the vote, knocking off John Carlin, the former governor.

With Newt Gingrich as the new Speaker of the House, I couldn't wait to get started in January of 1995. There was a lot on our agenda.

When we got going, we felt like we were changing the world, moving one piece of legislation forward after another. Welfare reform was a big one. We had to pass three different versions of the bill before cornering President Clinton to sign it.

As the head of "the New Federalists," the conservative wing of the '94 class, I was quoted in *Time*, *The Wall Street Journal*, and heck, even *The New York Times*.

Things couldn't have been better.

Or so I thought.

In reality, things couldn't have been much worse for my wife and family. All because of one individual, who hadn't been paying attention.

His initials: SB.

There was one sign after another. I just couldn't see any of them.

Like that time I called Mary from Pittsburg, Kansas, where I had given a speech on a Friday night. Another night on the road.

"Do you really need to be down there right now?" she asked. "You campaigned day and night for more than a year. Now you've been elected, and you're hardly ever home."

Even when I was home, I wasn't present, my mind swirling with thoughts of the next meeting, the next bill, the next press conference...the next whatever. This wasn't the life that Mary Margaret Stauffer had signed up for. She had expected to have a husband who came home after work, who coached Little League baseball. Who was there for his family.

Not long afterward, I left our family's summer vacation to speak at the Reform Party convention in Dallas.

Which shows how messed up my priorities had become. My kids were growing older—Abby, nine; Andy, seven; Elizabeth, five—and their father was AWOL. I let myself off the hook by saying I was doing important things for my state and my country. But that was no excuse. A lot of people do important things and still find the time to be there for their loved ones.

Truth is, I couldn't stop. I was addicted to my ambition.

As I walked through the marble hallways in Congress, gazing at the portraits of former legislators, people kept telling me how wonderful I was. I became so full of myself that I believed the right things wouldn't get done if I wasn't in the middle of it.

"Lord," I finally said one day in prayer, "You have got to change me because I am going the wrong way and I can't change myself."

A few days went by, then a few more, and I was still Selfish Sam.

It was maybe a week or so later that I noticed a brown mole on my side. I went to see a doctor. He took it off and sent it for a biopsy. I wasn't overly concerned.

Until the results of the biopsy came back: melanoma.

I was terrified.

I thought back to my father, who had been diagnosed with colon cancer in 1969. He made it through, but it was an early lesson in how fragile life truly is.

For weeks, I woke up in the middle of the night, wondering, *Is this it?*

As for God, I was a little bit ticked off. When I asked Him for a change, this wasn't exactly what I had in mind. As usual, though, it was exactly what I needed. Silly of me to question His plan.

It dawned on me: If this were, indeed, the end of my life, would I be happy with how I had lived? The answer was NO.

My life had been about me. God and my wife and family were in the room, but I was the one on the throne. I had willfully unhitched from my family to pursue my selfish goals. I would climb the mountain on my own, promising to come back and get them when I could. They would understand, since I was doing such important work.

Only there was always another mountain to climb. Another reason why the time wasn't right and I couldn't go back for them.

Soon after the surgery—the doctors took a large piece of flesh and muscle from my right side—I made one of the most important decisions of my life. A decision I should have made long before then.

I gave my life over to Jesus completely.

This was different from when I jumped off my dirt bike and got down on my knees.

Back then, I had allowed Jesus into my life, but I still wanted to be the one in control.

Oswald Chambers, an evangelist from the early twentieth century, referred to giving up the need for control and turning over everything you have to the Lord as "the white funeral." Better known as sanctification.

I got on my knees and told God, *I can't handle it anymore. I give You my life. You take care of it.*

I noticed the change right away. Not that I wasn't still flawed, quite flawed, but the change was that I stopped fussing about everything, stopped worrying about this meeting or that piece of legislation. I said to the Lord, *Whatever you want to do with my life, I'm good.*

The change was especially noticeable with my family. I was finally putting God first, my wife and children next, and politics a distant third. I called for a family meeting to apologize to everyone. My prayer time was also better. Before, I had seen Christ *for* me and, as the years went on, *in* me. Now, I saw Christ *through* me, my actions taking on the values and priorities He motivated in me. My time with the Lord went from a discipline I needed, similar to sit-ups or jogging, to the best part of my day.

I couldn't help wondering, *Why me? Why did God save my marriage while others in the Fellowship group I attended in Congress get divorced?*

His reply came through clearly: "You asked."

★ ★ ★

In 1996, after serving just one term in the House, I ran for the US Senate.

Blame Bob Dole.

Dole, my state's senior senator and the majority leader of the Senate, told me, "Some of you guys in the House ought to be thinking about running for the Senate."

I assumed he was referring to the seat held by Nancy Kassebaum, who was retiring after three terms.

Nope. He was referring to his seat.

Dole, who had been in the office since 1969, was going to resign in order to run against President Clinton in the '96 election as a private citizen; he had already secured the Republican nomination.

God had opened another gate for my wife and I and we walked through it.

Not that the race was going to be easy. This time, I would be running against the Republican Party establishment, which was backing Sheila Frahm, a moderate who filled the vacancy when Dole left. At one stage, I was nineteen points behind in the polls. A lot was on the line in the Republican primary. Lose, and I wouldn't just miss out on the Senate, I would be out of a job, period.

Even so, I felt no fear. I was following God's plan. Whatever happened, I would be at peace.

I beat Frahm in the primary by 13 points and won the general election over Jill Docking with nearly 54 percent of the vote.

Two years later, I was reelected to the full term of six years. I was excited to keep fighting for the issues at home and abroad that would determine our future as a nation.

One of the issues had to do with the People's Republic of China.

For the first time in a long time, there was reason for hope, the country showing signs of modernizing into a society with more freedom.

Hard to imagine these days, isn't it?

As mentioned before, I voted yes on granting Most Favored Nation status to China in 2000 and have regretted that vote ever since. More than almost any other vote in my whole career.

I wanted to believe China was changing. But in the end, it was all a well-staged lie. A Communist country is a Communist country, no matter how much makeup it might put on. I wasn't the only one to take the bait. Many of us in Congress were led to believe that economic growth, global engagement, and trade would make China more receptive to human rights, democracy, and the rule of law. That China, to put it simply, would become more like us. (I had been so certain of this outcome that when I served as a White House fellow during the George H. W. Bush administration in the early '90s, I made a bet with a classmate that within ten years China would be an Asian-style democracy. I lost that bet, needless to say.)

Some in Congress, including Frank Wolf (more on him in chapter 8), thought otherwise. Wolf had gone to China and

Tibet. He saw what the Chinese did to anyone who dared to defy the party.

I have revisited that vote often, and the guilt of being beguiled by China is part of what drives me to be so outspoken today. More importantly, though, in many years of human rights advocacy, I have seen the carnage the CCP has wrought. It must be stopped.

Before it's too late. Before China wins the war on faith.

I'm also motivated by how faith turned my life around—as a teenager, and then again as a grown man who finally realized the error of my ways. It disturbs me to no end to see people in other countries who aren't free to practice their religion, and it doesn't matter what religion it is or how strongly they believe in it.

This is a right every human being is entitled to, bar none. A right of the human soul.

In 2024, at the International Religious Freedom Summit in DC, which brings together people of faith from all over the world, a friend said something to me that I've thought about ever since: "All the experiences you've been through in public life have prepared you for this very moment."

To borrow from an occupation I grew up with, this is harvest time, when the crops are gathered. I'm relying on the knowledge, stature, and relationships that I have been blessed with during my decades of public service. I once heard that life moves at the speed of relationships. The deeper the relationship, the more that can be accomplished.

Truth be told, the cause of religious freedom was not on my mind when I arrived in Washington in January 1995.

I was focused on balancing the budget, reforming the tax system, and reducing abortions. And those would remain my priorities—until Sharon Payt joined my staff in early 1997. She had been involved in religious freedom work for a nongovernmental organization (NGO) and had troubling information about Christians who were being persecuted and imprisoned for their faith. I was unaware of this. I was familiar with the Jewish refuseniks in the days of the Soviet Union, but I didn't have a clue that there were others similar to them, and in all corners of the globe.

One day Sharon brought up a missionary in Uzbekistan (one of five nations in Central Asia that had broken away from the Soviet Union in the early 1990s) who was in jail for no other reason than he was a Christian and was spreading the Gospel.

"I think that if we write a letter to the president of Uzbekistan, it might get him better treatment," Sharon suggested. "Or, at the very least, they might not kill him."

I wrote the letter and didn't think much of it. A few weeks later, while I was attending one of my kids' softball games, Sharon called.

The missionary in Uzbekistan had been let go.

I couldn't believe it. I had gotten excited about some of the victories during my early years in Congress, but this one was special. The man wasn't only kept alive but set free. I want to do more of this, I told my staff, a lot more. As the years went on, I had the same feeling every time we were successful. Sometimes it took longer than expected. We worked on one case for ten years before the person was released. And there were other occasions—too many—on which we weren't successful: The persecuted person was left in prison or came down with a "strange illness" and passed away. I was deeply troubled every time.

I still run into people in Washington that I helped get out of jail. To see them free and, in many instances, working to get others out, warms my soul like you wouldn't believe.

The fight for religious freedom reminds me of another Kansan who tried to liberate men and women in captivity—the famous abolitionist John Brown.

I know what you're thinking:

Wasn't John Brown the guy who was executed for inciting a slave rebellion and killing a bunch of innocent people at Harpers Ferry, the federal arsenal in Virginia?

He was, indeed, and I'm not about to defend murder. Under any circumstance.

As a matter of fact, when I was a boy and first heard about Brown, who led anti-slavery volunteers in the 1856 uprising known as Bleeding Kansas (my mom, incidentally, grew up on the property where Brown once lived), I thought he was too wild. An image of him on the wall in the State Capitol in Topeka shows Brown holding a Bible in one hand and a rifle in another, with his hair on fire and a dead Union soldier and a dead Confederate soldier lying at his feet.

Years later, however, disgusted with how African-Americans were treated in our country, slavery being our national sin, my view of him changed dramatically. Brown "felt their chains" while others, in the North as well as the South, felt nothing for the slaves. He was moved to action to free his fellow man. His passion for others wouldn't let him rest until every slave was freed.

Again, I'm not condoning how Brown dealt with those injustices, but the passion that burned inside him burns inside many people who fight against the gross injustice of religious persecution. And that's the kind of fire we need to end this nightmare.

★ ★ ★

In 1997, during a Bible study for members of the Senate, Dr. Lloyd Ogilvie, the Senate chaplain, posed a question I didn't expect.

"How many constituents do you have?" he asked the dozen or so of us in the group.

Easy question. Everyone responded quickly.

If you are a member of the US Senate, you know how many constituents you have, what they are interested in, and what it will take to get reelected.

He said all of us were wrong.

"Each of you has just one constituent," Dr. Ogilvie said, "and that constituent is God. If God is happy with what you're doing and the measures you're supporting in the Senate, then everything is going to be fine. But if He isn't happy, none of this is going to matter."

I walked out of that Bible study pondering what he had told us. Was my entire idea of public service based on the wrong approach?

From the day I took my oath before God, I had thought of the nearly three million constituents throughout my state, wondering how I could satisfy one group without alienating another, a nearly impossible undertaking. After the challenge from the chaplain, however, I began to pray over what God would want me to concentrate on. I still worked hard to lower taxes, balance the budget, and provide for our military, but I also became heavily involved in what, according to Scripture, God values—things like caring for the poor and the helpless.

By following the Lord, I was certain I would be doing more for the people of Kansas than ever. God is the Author of life. He will make sure I do right by Him and the good people of Kansas. And that is the mindset I maintained the rest of my years in the Senate and as governor and as the US ambassador-at-large for international religious freedom.

Which brings me to our challenge today: liberating those who are being persecuted in the People's Republic of China. It's not just China I worry about; it's also, as I can't explain often enough, the totalitarian system China is spreading around the world, and the danger it poses to freedom.

In 1995, when I was still in my cancer scare, I was up late one night at my home in Topeka.

I felt the urge to take my resume out of the drawer. I looked it over, as I had done many times in the past.

It had served as a source of pride, a testament to me and my accomplishments. On this night, however, it served as a source of shame.

It was a reminder of the person I had become, driven by earthly pursuits. Everything on the resume, I realized, would eventually burn up and what I needed to focus on for the rest of my days was touching souls in a way that would help them eternally.

I emptied the trash can, took out a match and burned the resume. I threw away the other copies, as well. I haven't compiled a full resume ever since.

I felt free. I didn't know what would lie ahead, but I knew I would be available to my loving Father and whatever challenges He would have for me.

The challenge He has for me now, and for many of us, is the struggle for religious freedom in China. And throughout the world.

Our challenge is enormous, to be sure, but it is one God has prepared us for with all His grace.

CHAPTER 3

THE NEW MAYFLOWER CHURCH

PASTOR PAN YONGGUANG, NOW FORTY-EIGHT years old, didn't think much about faith during the first twenty-plus years of his life. He thought about success. About how to make something of himself. Whenever someone brought up the subject of religion, he asked a few questions and quickly moved on to less heavenly matters.

Yongguang had nothing against the people who were true believers. It's just that he wasn't one of them.

Then, in 2000, came the accident. His father, who had taught him so much and had such high expectations for him, was hit by a truck while riding a bicycle. In the hospital there was nothing Yongguang could do. Except wait and worry. And watch as members of his sister's church prayed for his father's recovery. Yongguang was deeply touched. He had never witnessed such love. For a complete stranger, no less.

His father, only forty-four years old, never regained consciousness. The damage to his brain was too severe. He died the day after the accident.

Not long afterward, Yongguang quit his job—he had been a surgeon, mostly repairing fractures of arms and legs—and moved from Yunfu, a city of two million in the western province of

Guangdong, to Shenzhen, the sixth most populous city in China, to take care of his paternal grandmother, who was a widow. He found administrative work in a local company. Every so often, when his sister came by to visit, she brought up the teachings of the Gospel.

As usual, he asked questions. This time, he thought about the answers. A lot.

After his grandmother passed away, Yongguang began attending the Wanfeng Church, where his sister worshipped, becoming friendly with a pastor from Hong Kong who served as his mentor. It was also where he learned how to pray and met his future wife.

On Easter Sunday 2003, Pan Yongguang was baptized. Two years later, after training under pastors affiliated with a US-based Reformed Presbyterian church, he was no longer Pan Yongguang.

He was Pastor Pan.

His mother wasn't pleased. Her son was giving up a job with status and prospects, a future. For what? To lead others in prayer?

In her mind, the son she knew was dead.

"How can I expect you to take care of me when I'm old?" she asked him. "It looks like I will have to take care of you."

The Wanfeng Church, which had about eighty members, held weekly services and classes in rented office space. It was a "house church," operating on the model that Peter Xu had helped develop throughout China. Over the last twenty-five years, since Peter was released from jail in China and came to the United States, house churches have represented the largest growth of Christians in Asia.

Their allegiance is to Jesus Christ.

Not to Xi Jinping.

God bless them.

★ ★ ★

By the spring of 2019, Pastor Pan, now head of the Shenzhen Holy Reformed Church he had founded seven years earlier, was beginning to wonder, *Is it safe to remain in China?*

The CCP was monitoring his church and other house churches more closely than ever, police officers often showing up in the middle of his sermons. Sometimes they took him to a restaurant for questioning, sometimes to the police station. The goal was to intimidate him with one hostile question after another: *What have you been doing lately? What is your church up to?* Things like that.

Pastor Pan told the truth. With their army of spies and constant surveillance, they knew everything anyway.

The authorities put pressure on his landlord, as well, forcing Pastor Pan and his family to search for a new home.

One time, the officers confiscated Bibles and hymn books from church members. A young girl asked the pastor afterward if he could get them back. He said he couldn't. He felt awful about letting her down.

Pastor Pan didn't interrupt his sermons when the children were noisy, but whenever he heard a knock on the door, he stopped immediately, turning his attention toward the front of the room, as did other members of the church.

Was it someone they knew or was it the police? Usually the police.

The church members were ready. Pastor Pan had prepared them with a series of drills.

"Don't take out weapons or anything sharp," he told them. "Take out your phone and point it at the intruders. Shame them."

Not that it ever did much good.

On at least two occasions, the entire congregation was brought to the police station. Most of the time, however, only Pastor Pan and a few of the elders were taken away, always the same officer in charge.

I asked if he grew to hate the officer.

No, he did not hate him. He pitied him. He even asked others to pray for him. The man was simply a cog in the system. I like to believe I would have been as forgiving as Pastor Pan, but I can't be certain.

In other instances, the officer told him, "We are not here to take you. Just to take pictures and understand the position you are in. You can continue with your service."

How gracious of him.

The harassment never shocked Pastor Pan. From the moment he organized a house church, he knew the harassment was coming and it was a price he was willing to pay.

For Pastor Pan, the intense scrutiny started in 2018, after the arrest of his friend and fellow pastor Wang Yi and the closing of Pastor Wang's Early Rain Covenant Church. Pastor Pan was among the approximately four hundred church leaders who signed a letter written by Wang Yi that objected to new regulations tightening the oversight on religious activities and funding. (I will be telling you more about Pastor Wang in the next chapter.)

Not long afterward came the pro-democracy protests in Hong Kong, which is only twenty-five miles from Shenzhen.

Shenzhen was similar to Hong Kong in many respects—lifestyle, food, customs, language, and so forth. So when the Chinese cracked down in Hong Kong, everyone became anxious that Shenzhen would be next.

As the terror and fear unfolded, Pastor Pan began to have serious doubts. About himself.

"God," he said in his prayers, "I'm not the person to do this. I'm not Wang Yi."

Pastor Pan was scared of being arrested, of disappearing for good like so many others. And, perhaps more scared of not being the strong, confident leader the members of his church desperately needed. Their freedom—their lives!—were on the line.

For weeks, he and the members of his church spoke to one another and prayed about what they should do.

Some of them wanted to stay in China. China was their home. It was all they knew, and if they left, who was to say they would ever be able to return? Besides, what kind of work would they find anywhere else? They had secure jobs in China, many at factories.

Others saw no alternative to getting out. What kind of home was it if they couldn't practice their faith? Their children were in a church-run school, studying the Bible. What if they were forced to yield to the increasing pressure from the CCP to send them to state-run schools where they would be brainwashed with atheism and Marxism? (As we'll see in chapters 7 and 11, education is a powerful tool in China's campaign to suppress religion, including Tibetan Buddhism and the Uyghurs' Muslim faith. The Communists appear to have discovered that the systematic education of religious minorities' children in their ideology is more effective than the violent persecution of the faithful.)

The Shenzhen Holy Reformed Church, like other house churches under siege, moved from one place of worship to another. That was the beauty of not having a building of its own. All it needed was a Bible, a hymn book, and a group of believers. Even a public park would do. Pastor Pan thanked God that his flock was unencumbered by earthly possessions.

In the fall of 2019, the church members, meeting in a cramped rented office space, took a vote. The decision was fifty-seven to seventeen to leave China.

At first they thought of sending out just the younger folks—more than half of the congregation were minors—but ultimately decided to make the move as a whole church. It was the Holy Spirit, Pastor Pan told me, that was urging them to go. I don't doubt it for a second.

Only, to go where, precisely?

Not America. No one thought that was remotely possible. Including Pastor Pan.

They chose Jeju Island on the southern tip of South Korea.

Jeju Island? I had never heard of it, either.

The reason was that most church members didn't have visas, and Jeju Island, a popular destination for Chinese tourists, was one of the few places you could travel to without one.

They started their exodus in October 2019. Pastor Pan was one of the first to go, though he had to be extremely careful. A few months earlier, he had booked a ticket to attend a theological conference in Thailand, but shortly before he was to depart, he received a call from the Chinese authorities.

"We know you are planning to go to Thailand," they told him, "but you can't go."

"I'm going," he pushed back. "You can't stop me."

This was from someone who wondered whether he possessed enough courage to lead his church. Please.

Anyway, on the day he was scheduled to travel, two police officers showed up at his front door.

So much for the conference in Thailand.

He couldn't afford to be stopped like that again. Not with everyone depending on him.

This time, he didn't book his tickets—for a boat to Hong Kong and then a plane from Hong Kong to Jeju Island—until the last possible minute. If he had purchased his tickets any earlier, the agent surveilling him would have been able to alert the customs officials at the border which, in all likelihood, would have ended any possibility of Pastor Pan and the members of his church ever leaving China. And maybe even put him in prison.

The other members of the church made separate plans. They didn't have many possessions—no houses or cars—and that was to their advantage.

Fewer items to pack. Fewer loose ends to tie up. Fewer chances to attract unwelcome attention.

Some needed more time to prepare, mainly to say goodbye to family members they knew they would probably never see again.

Unfortunately, a few waited too long. Once Covid hit in early 2020, they had to remain in China. Which is where they remain today. It breaks my heart when I imagine what their lives must be like.

Once he was safe in South Korea, Pastor Pan, who had yet to apply for refugee status, was required to leave the country every thirty days. Each time, he went to Hong Kong—he didn't dare to leave the airport—and flew back to Jeju Island the following day.

During those monthly trips, he preached online to church members who had yet to leave China. (The Chinese had built a firewall around their internet that kept him from doing that from South Korea.)

On one occasion, a female church member who was still in China said, "Pastor, I think you have abandoned us."

Pastor Pan, a sensitive soul, became extremely sad. For a couple of hours he sat at the airport, trying to figure out what to do. Then it came to him: He would go back to China. He would prove to her and other stranded members of his flock that he wasn't abandoning them. No matter what the risks might be to him personally.

But on his way to the ticket counter, he accidentally kicked a woman's suitcase.

"Are you blind?" the woman shouted.

Pastor Pan saw it as a sign from God. He was being blind, all right—by even *thinking* about returning to the country that wouldn't allow him to be God's faithful servant.

He went to the restroom and broke down. And never gave the idea of going back another thought.

As for Covid, it worked both ways.

While keeping some church members in China, it also, thank God, prevented others from returning home when their lives in South Korea weren't turning out as well as they had hoped. "This isn't the road I wanted to travel," one church member told *The Wall Street Journal* in tears as she talked about working in the fields in the rain and snow. "Sometimes I think, 'How great was my life in China? My husband could support us, I could lie around doing nothing if I wanted. Why do I have to suffer like this?'"[5] Prior to the world shutting down, some members became so disillusioned that they did, indeed, go back to China, including Pastor Pan's sister—who, you may recall, first showed him the meaning of faith.

Does she regret going back? I asked Pastor Pan. I saw the sadness in his eyes. He didn't have to answer.

The epidemic also meant the CCP couldn't send its spies to Jeju Island. If the government agents who had been surveilling Pastor Pan and his church had been able to travel freely, who knows how differently things might have turned out?

In any case, they were no longer known as the Shenzhen Holy Reformed Church.

They were now the Mayflower Church, renamed for the English ship that carried the Pilgrims to the New World in pursuit of religious freedom in 1620.

The Pilgrims were Protestant Christians, too, and just like the members of the Mayflower Church, they weren't about to let their children be torn away from their faith. They fled to Holland to escape persecution by the English state church, but when they found it impossible to pass their faith along to their children there, they sailed to America, the New World. Before they landed at Plymouth Rock, Massachusetts, they signed the Mayflower Compact, establishing their own system of government.

The Mayflower Church members adapted to their new surroundings in South Korea as well as could be expected. They got jobs. They had babies. They were free to worship the God they loved, using space lent to them by a local church.

But Jeju Island would not be the permanent solution to their troubles.

In the summer of 2022, the pandemic was easing up, which meant more flights coming in from China. More flights and more security officials.

There were also more phone calls.

"This is a warning," a voice on the other end of the line would say. "What you are doing is illegal and you are threatening Chinese national security. You have to go back to China."

The church members were "invited" to the Chinese consular office, which reminded them of the times back home they were "invited" to the police station "to drink tea."

There was no drinking tea, of course. The calls were nothing more than a ruse to get them to show up.

Before long, whenever church members saw calls coming from the Chinese consular office on Jeju Island, they didn't answer the phone.

Meanwhile, in China, their relatives were being constantly harassed. Many, no doubt forced to do so by the authorities, pleaded with their loved ones to return.

Pastor Pan was in the greatest danger. He was advised to hide in a different place from his family and avoid contact with his congregation.

Fat chance of that happening.

"One evening," he recalled in an interview with *Plough,* a magazine published by the Bruderhof Christian community, "my wife and I took a walk and didn't return at the agreed time. My son and daughter cried and prayed; they thought their parents had been arrested."[6]

Meanwhile, the members of the Mayflower Church applied for asylum in South Korea but were rejected by the government. No surprise there. In 2020, according to Nancen, a refugee rights center in Seoul, of the thousands of refugee applications submitted, only 0.4 percent were granted.

Which got me thinking: Isn't South Korea a democracy? Doesn't it allow the freedom of religion?

Yes—and no.

While it appears to be accommodating to the West, South Korea, similar to many countries, goes out of its way to avoid angering China, its most lucrative trade partner.

In any case, the possibility became very real that the South Korean government might send the Mayflower Church members back to China once every legal avenue had been exhausted.

Which led to the obvious question: Where could they go now?

One option was Hungary. Except Hungary didn't want to antagonize China. Taking in a handful of refugees might have been acceptable. But an entire church? No way.

Once the church members started to consider Thailand, the discussions become quite contentious.

What about the women who were pregnant? Could they make it there safely? What about those whose passports had expired? Without any legal status, what kind of jobs could they land? (In South Korea, many worked in the fields, picking radishes, cabbages, and tangerines. They didn't earn much money, but it was better than nothing.)

And what if only some church members could get into Thailand?

The group had been through so much together. The idea that they might be separated was terrifying.

One woman who had a newborn and thought the journey would be too risky accused Pastor Pan of abandoning them.

The pastor was heartbroken, as he had been when the church member in China made the same accusation. A few days later, he delivered a sermon that explained why Thailand was, indeed, where they needed to go. He asked everyone to sign a statement he drafted which he referred to as the New Mayflower Compact.

Everyone did.

"In the name of God," the statement said, "by His grace and for His glory, we the undersigned members of the New Mayflower Church, solemnly pledge our commitment. Our purpose is to promote and preserve the faith in Christ, safeguarding it from the influence of atheistic education. We acknowledge the imminent danger and lack of legal status in our current location, which has led us to make a resolute decision to embark on a new journey."

So, in the summer of 2022, after nearly three years on Jeju Island, they took off for Thailand.

Where they would be in more peril than ever.

★ ★ ★

As Pastor Pan recounted each detail of the journey, I kept wondering, *Why didn't my own country, the beacon of freedom around the world, take the worshippers in?*

I posed the question to Bob Fu, the head of ChinaAid, an organization based in Midland, Texas, that provides legal assistance to persecuted Christians and human rights defenders.

Bob, who could be a whole chapter himself, was a student leader during the Tiananmen Square demonstrations in 1989. Which cost him his livelihood—a teacher, he wasn't permitted to pursue his Master's degree—but led to a life more fulfilling than he ever could have imagined. "Because of that experience and the persecution after that," Bob told me, "I was called, believing in Jesus as my Savior and Lord." He and his wife, Heidi, who were both imprisoned in Beijing in 1996 for "illegal evangelism," were very fortunate to get out of China later the same year.

I can't imagine how the Mayflower Church would have gotten along without Bob's advice and the funds he raised. Several Korean churches also donated clothes and inexpensive vehicles to help after church members had depleted much of their limited life savings.

Bob said that the goal, naturally, was to resettle the Mayflower Church in the United States. But for that to happen, the Biden administration would need to believe there was an "imminent threat" to the safety of the church members, and that threshold apparently had not been met.

I was appalled. Of course there was an imminent threat. Chinese spies and agents were everywhere in Thailand.

One day, Pastor Pan and another pastor spotted two Chinese men in a restaurant videotaping them.

"You can't do that," the other pastor told them.

"We are just tourists," they claimed. "We're videotaping the restaurant."

The lack of action by the White House reminded me of the MS *St. Louis*, the German ship, filled with nearly a thousand Jewish refugees, that attempted to flee from the Nazis in 1939. The US didn't let them in, and the ship sailed from off the Florida coast back to Europe. Many of the passengers later died in the concentration camps. President Roosevelt was a strong leader during the war years, but the *St. Louis* episode was shameful, to put it mildly.

I know one thing: If I had been the ambassador-at-large for international religious freedom in 2022, I would have thrown a fit.

At this point Pastor Pan was thinking, *If the US doesn't come to our aid, and soon, there is no hope.* No wonder he experienced some serious health issues (high blood pressure, stomach pains, and so forth) after a couple of months in Thailand.

God, he said in his prayers, *please let me guide these people to the Promised Land and you can take me away after that.* By the "Promised Land," he meant America.

Which brings us to late March 2023.

Every time I think of what happened—and what could have happened—I want to shout to the heavens or cry my eyes out.

On March 30, Thai police officers arrived at a compound in the city of Pattaya, less than one hundred miles from Bangkok, where the church members were staying. No one had been expecting the police. They asked for everyone's passports and for the entire group to gather outside, in temperatures close to 100 degrees. There were several pickup trucks, along with extra security officials and immigration police. The situation was becoming more dire by the second.

The church members were loaded onto the pickup trucks and driven to the Pattaya Immigration Bureau, where they suddenly found themselves in a court proceeding. The officers asked them for money to secure their release and then changed their mind, instructing everyone to sign some documents.

Fortunately, Pastor Pan was in contact with Bob Fu, who told him not to sign a thing. Bob was concerned that the Mayflower Church members would sign what amounted to voluntary repatriation agreements.

They spent the night at the immigrant detention center.

The next day, after paying a small fine, they got on two buses to take them back to the compound. At least, that's what they believed...until they noticed that the buses, instead of turning onto a side road to Pattaya, were picking up speed and heading on the highway toward Bangkok. Then they saw a sign for Bangkok's Suvarnabhumi Airport, about an hour and a half away.

Which could mean only one thing: The Mayflower Church was on its way back to China.

When Pastor Pan told Bob about the sign and where the buses were headed, he couldn't have been more emphatic: "Do whatever you can do to stop that bus." That prompted a number of the church members (they had been taking photos and videos to send to Bob and anyone else they knew of who might be able to help) to rush toward the front of the bus.

They had nothing to lose. They were sure they would die if they got on the plane to China.

Somehow, they persuaded the driver to stop the buses and let them out for a short break. They climbed over a roadside barrier and onto the grass.

And that's when it happened: a display of amazing courage, and, if you don't mind me suggesting, divine intervention.

Her name is Chen Jingjing, a former factory worker. She was thirty-three years old at the time. And pregnant. When she realized a Thai policeman was about to beat up Pastor Pan, something in her snapped.

Maybe it was the baby she was carrying. Maybe the toll of three and a half years on the run. Who knows?

Whatever it was, Chen—all of five feet and a couple of inches tall—inserted herself between the officer and Pastor Pan and raised her hands.

"You're not going to hurt a pregnant woman, are you?" she said.

No, thank goodness, he was not.

Meanwhile, Bob Fu was working the phones in Texas like never before. He sent emails to everyone in and out of government—including the State Department, Senator Ted Cruz, and House members Chris Smith and Mike McCaul—that he had been in touch with in recent days about the dangers facing the church members.

The subject header for the emails: "SOS, Mayflower Church hijacked."

Fortunately, two Americans were on the buses along with the Mayflower Church members: Deana Brown, the head of Freedom Seekers International, based in Tyler, Texas, which assists in the resettlement of persecuted Christians around the world, and Stacy Nichols, a member of the nearby Flint Baptist Church. Which, according to Bob, was instrumental in motivating the

State Department and other officials to move faster in finding a diplomatic solution.

I don't know precisely what happened over the next couple of hours, nor does Bob Fu. All I'm sure of is that Secretary of State Antony Blinken, with help from others, was able to persuade the Thai officials, who no doubt had been pressured by the Chinese, to change their mind.

The buses wouldn't go to the airport. They would go back to the immigration detention center.

"You can get back on the bus," Bob assured Pastor Pan.

I wonder, *What if Chen Jingjing hadn't shown such courage?* What she did kept the church members off the bus for an hour, maybe longer, a delay that was essential in giving Blinken enough time to negotiate with the Thai authorities.

A week later, the sixty-four members of the Mayflower Church received the incredible news: The United States of America would grant them asylum. Like the Israelites led out of Egypt by Moses, they were on their way to the Promised Land. The significance of the number sixty-four was not lost on Pastor Pan—6/4 (June 4) being the day in 1989 when the Chinese suppressed the demonstration at Tiananmen Square.

As they departed the detention center in Thailand, the pastor led the group in singing the words of Psalm 126: "When the Lord restored the fortunes of Zion, we were like those who dreamed. Our mouths were filled with laughter, our tongues with songs of joy. Then it was said among nations, 'The Lord has done great things for them.'"[7]

Everyone cried, including some of the guards.

"Then the consul issued us vias," Pastor Pan told *Plough*. "As I held mine, I thought of the movie *Schindler's List* and thanked the U.S. government for including everyone in the Mayflower Church on its list. Boarding the plane to the United States, I still couldn't believe that what had happened was real."[8]

I wish I had been at Dulles International Airport just outside Washington, DC, when Pastor Pan and the other church members got off the plane from Thailand.

To see the happiness and relief on their faces. And to see these wonderful servants of God have a chance to live their lives, finally, in peace and not fear. From Dulles they flew to Dallas, setting up a new home in Tyler before settling, eventually, in Midland.

Of course, it would take quite a while for their fears to go away completely.

During one of Pastor Pan's sermons in Texas, a police officer entered the church. Pastor Pan stopped immediately, and the whole congregation turned around. Like the old days in China. He reminded everyone, and himself, they were in America now. The officer was there to protect them.

★ ★ ★

In May 2025, I flew to Midland to meet with Bob Fu, Pastor Pan, and the members of the Mayflower Church.

What I witnessed will remain with me for the rest of my life.

At first glance, their new home didn't look like much, just a few nondescript metal buildings at the end of a dusty road.

The middle of nowhere.

Not a very auspicious place for the Mayflower Church to make harbor, I thought to myself.

Then I walked into one of the buildings for a potluck dinner. The scene was electric, full of joy, laughter, and peace. Kids were running around, laughing, playing, being kids. I couldn't hear myself think, and I wouldn't have wanted it any other way.

I gazed at the adults in the room and saw the same happiness. The same love. The same commitment to each other. This was their home, their church, their family. They were free now to practice their faith…in a dusty oil field in Texas. Things had looked dismal from the outside, but what I witnessed on the inside could not have been more golden.

Before dinner, Pastor Pan led everyone in prayer. As he had in China, South Korea, and Thailand.

Their prayers had come true. Against overwhelming odds.

A part of me was not surprised that they were rescued.

As it says in the Bible, God "strongly support[s] those whose heart is completely His."[9]

After dinner, I spoke with Chen Jingjing. She was holding her daughter Monica on her lap. The one who was in her womb when she stood between the Thai police and Pastor Pan. Monica was named after the mother of Augustine of Hippo, a Christian theologian from the fourth and fifth centuries.

I asked Chen what she considered the greatest blessing she has received from the Lord.

"Through the biggest trials, the biggest events," she told me through an interpreter, "I have gotten to know God better and have gained faith."

I also spoke with Pastor Pan. I wondered if he recognized himself as a man of courage, and that's when he opened up about his inner doubts.

As the conversation went on, he had more to say on the subject.

"Perhaps you can say that it is courage," he conceded, "but it comes from the responsibility that has been put on me from God and the trust that others have in me."

His wish for the Mayflower Church, which currently uses the First Baptist Church's chapel and youth center for its prayer services—other churches in the region have contributed with housing, transportation, and food—is to be financially independent and have their own permanent place of worship.

And to stay together. As a church and community.

The Pilgrims on the Mayflower, he told *Plough*, "lived in a community for twenty-four years before they separated.... This is the direction I am working toward, because Jesus wants his saints to be gathered together."[10]

Whether they stay together or not—modern life is full of temptations—they were together when it mattered most.

"The whole thing was like being in a dream," Pastor Pan said.

CHAPTER 4

THE MARTIN LUTHER KING JR. OF CHINA

I MET WANG YI ONCE, when I was in the Senate. But it was brief meeting, and so much has happened since then.

To the struggle for religious freedom. And to the man himself.

Wang Yi, the pastor of the Early Rain Covenant Church, has been in prison since late 2018, with his sentence not due to end until December 2027. Some observers doubt whether he will be released then.

When I met him in June 2006, he was a prominent human rights lawyer visiting DC. with two other Chinese activists to meet with President George W. Bush and a few top advisers in the White House. I can't overstate how critical the meeting was for the cause we were all fighting for. No sitting US president had ever met with members of a house church. Bush was always intent on letting the leadership in China—and perhaps more important, the Chinese people themselves—know that even the president of the United States believes in God.

Wang Yi and the others briefed Bush on the latest events back home, and as the meeting was about to wrap up, the president, a man of deep faith, said to everyone, *Let's hold hands and pray.*

The group bowed their heads in prayer. It must have been a special moment.

How I wish I were able to see Wang Yi again.

In good health and among those who share his commitment to Jesus Christ. Where he belongs.

There would be no end to my questions:

What led you to your conversion to Christ?

What persuaded you to switch from law to a full-time pastor?

How were you able to keep up your spirits all the years you were in prison?

How should the Church in China, more besieged than ever, move forward?

Wang Yi, now fifty-two, reminds me a great deal of Peter Xu. Both men are at total peace, even when they encounter the most dire circumstances. God sure knows how to pick them, doesn't He?

"This Communist regime's persecution against the church is a greatly wicked, unlawful action," Wang Yi wrote in an incredibly powerful letter, "My Declaration of Faithful Disobedience," which he had arranged to be released forty-eight hours after his arrest. "The calling that I have received requires me to use non-violent methods to disobey those human laws that disobey the Bible and God. My Savior Christ also requires me to joyfully bear all costs for disobeying wicked laws."

I have gone over the letter numerous times. It is incredible. One part, among many that stand out, is the word *joyfully.* Wang Yi was joyful because he knew he was obeying the only laws that mattered. The laws of Heaven, not the government.

Wang Yi's letter sounds a lot like what Peter Xu said to the warden after they took him off His cross.

Little wonder that Wang Yi is considered by many the Martin Luther King Jr. of China.

In 1963, Dr. King, who had been arrested after leading a nonviolent protest in Birmingham, Alabama, penned his powerful "Letter from Birmingham Jail," in which he stated, "Injustice anywhere is a threat to justice everywhere. We are caught in an inescapable network of mutuality, tied in a single garment of destiny. Whatever affects one directly affects all indirectly."

Amen.

★ ★ ★

Like countless others of his generation, Wang Yi, who was sixteen at the time, was profoundly affected by Tiananmen Square. According to Xi Lian, a professor of world Christianity at Duke, the massacre resulted in many expressing a "complete disillusionment with communist rule and the leaders of China. There was nothing to fill the vacuum of belief. They began to search for a new world view that would give their life meaning."[11] Soon after Tiananmen Square, Wang Yi was preparing to mimeograph and distribute articles about the massacre among his fellow high school students when his father found out and put an end to it. Later on, as a pastor, he held a prayer meeting every year on June 4 for the victims. "Many people ask us why we pray for June 4th as it is politics. I…didn't see politics, I saw people getting killed, an injustice, people being oppressed and suffering. In a politicized society, just maintaining freedom of conscience is already considered political." [12]

Teaching law at Chengdu University in the province of Sichuan was his first full-time job. He got to see a number of human rights cases up close.

In 1992, shortly before he took his college entrance exam, Wang Yi began to date a woman by the name of Jiang Rong. The two had gone to the same kindergarten, primary school, and middle school, but they didn't really get to know each other until their senior year of high school.

While Jiang attended Chongqing University, eleven hours away by train, they exchanged about eight hundred letters. If that's not being in love, I don't know what it is. They got married in 1997.

Writing has always been in Wang Yi's blood: poems, essays, movie reviews, you name it.

In the early 2000s, he became a columnist for *China News Weekly* and put out a book of his writings. One publication listed him among China's fifty most influential public intellectuals. Which, not surprisingly, prompted the CCP to issue a decree that kept him from being published in the state-owned press. His website was also shut down. Yet he would not be silenced. "Of course it matters," he said, "that the microphone was taken way. But vocal cords are part of one's body. And the right to speak is an inalienable one—one which is laid down in black and white in China's constitution."[13]

So, never having the chance to ask him myself, I asked others what led Wang Yi to convert to Christianity in 2005—his wife had been baptized a year before—and begin a fellowship in his home that would become known as the Early Rain Reformed Church, and later, the Early Rain Covenant Church. The church, which would eventually grow to eight hundred members, contained a seminary and primary school and supported the families of political prisoners.

Two cases, I was told, had a huge impact on him.

The first, in 2001, involved Gong Shengliang, founder of the South China Church, which, with a reported fifty thousand members, was labeled by the CCP as a cult. He was sentenced to death, though the Chinese, bowing to pressure from overseas, commuted the sentence to life imprisonment and subsequently to nineteen years' imprisonment. Wang Yi was deeply moved by members of the South China Church who, while being tortured, refused to bear witness against other Christians.

The second case related to Cai Zhuohua, a pastor at a house church in Beijing, who was detained in 2004 for possessing a large number of Bibles and other religious items.

★ ★ ★

The transition Wang Yi was making is easy to understand. Christianity, after all, provides a religious foundation for democracy with its fundamental view that every human being has a right to be free and that we are all equal in the eyes of the Lord. And being children of God means we are "endowed by [our] Creator with certain unalienable rights." Those rights don't just apply to Americans. They are the rights of all people, including the Chinese.

Around this time, Wang Yi received a sign from God. He was looking for a book on the shelf one day when he fell off the stool he was standing on and couldn't get up. He remained on the floor for hours until his wife arrived and took him to the hospital.

The sign was unmistakable: Books, which symbolized rationality and knowledge, were not superior to faith.

Prior to then, he had attended meetings about the Gospel at his home, but there were still doubts in his heart.

There would never be doubts again.

One person I spoke to said the questions that Wang Yi began to ask himself were issues that could not be addressed by a lawyer. They had to do with the most pressing question we all face: our eternal destiny.

In 2008, Wang Yi quit his job at the university. He founded the Early Rain Reformed Church and began serving as its pastor. That's something that makes him unique. A lot of human rights lawyers turn to Christ. Very few take the next step and become a pastor.

He came to the conclusion after an earthquake of 7.9 magnitude on May 12, 2008, struck Sichuan, the worst in China since 1976.

Nearly seventy thousand people died, mostly from collapsed buildings and landslides, and almost four hundred thousand were injured. Wang Yi saw more clearly than ever the fragility of life, the impermanence of our earthly dwelling, and the urgency of saving souls through the Gospel. The church became a receiving station for Christians who were arriving in Chengdu to give aid. From then on at his church, May 12 would be a day of prayer for the nation.

In his second career, Wang Yi hasn't shied away from politics. Which hasn't gone over well with some pastors among China's house churches, who feel the focus should always be on theology. But leaning heavily on Western political thought, he has written and spoken a great deal about the rights of the individual.

Not a big leap, I suppose, for a former human rights lawyer.

Fast-forward to a sermon Wang Yi gave in May 2018.

He had been planning the annual memorial service for victims of the earthquake.

The police had other plans.

They picked Wang Yi up and detained him for twenty-four hours. They also took away dozens of others who had shown up for the service, and confiscated publications belonging to the church.

At the police station, Wang Yi was forced to take everything off. Including his wedding ring.

"It felt like the chief priest going into the most holy place—he had to leave behind all his belongings and relationships, because he must face the Lord by himself," he explained in a sermon two days later.[14]

He was calm. Unlike the earlier times he was detained.

"I was able to put everything aside all of a sudden," he said.[15]

The sermon he gave that Sunday was one of his most memorable.

"When I was in the police station yesterday," he told the members of his church..."I thought about what is in front of us, and how I did not know we had been preparing for this over the past two years. I was certain of one thing: As long as this church is still proclaiming the Gospel, as long as God's Word is still in the mouths and hearts of our brothers and sisters, this church cannot be destroyed."[16]

In September 2018, as mentioned earlier, more than four hundred pastors from across China, including Pastor Pan of the Mayflower Church, signed a letter, known as "Declaration for the Sake of the Christian Faith," Wang Yi drafted in response to a broad government decree implemented in February of that year that restricted virtually every aspect of religious activities. For instance, anyone under the age of eighteen wasn't permitted to attend church. Traveling abroad to Christian conferences was banned, as well, and those who failed to comply with any of the restrictions would be arrested.

"We believe," the statement read, "that these unjust actions are an abuse of government power and have led to serious conflicts between political and religious parties in Chinese society. These actions infringe on the human freedoms of religion and conscience and violate the universal rule of law.... God hates all attempts to suppress human souls and all acts of persecution against the Christian Church."[17]

Around the same time, Wang Yi gave another sermon to remember.

I can't believe what he said. And I can't think of anyone else in China who would have had the courage to say it.

"When we are not being persecuted, we spread the Gospel," Wang Yi preached. "And when persecution comes, we continue spreading the Gospel."

And then...

"If we are talking about a president, we declare he is a sinner. And if we are talking about a general secretary, we still declare he is a sinner. We believe that we have the responsibility to tell Xi Jinping that he is a sinner. The government he is leading has sinned greatly against God...and if he does not repent, he will perish!"[18]

From then on, it was only a matter of time before the Chinese Communists would put Wang Yi away, and he knew it. Come to think of it, he had always known the day was coming.

He deliberately gained a lot of weight, certain he would lose a lot once he was incarcerated.

He also began to memorize as many Bible verses and hymns as he could, realizing it was likely the authorities wouldn't give him a Bible or prayer book.

And held meetings with his co-workers to discuss contingency plans.

The day came soon enough.

On December 9, 2018, the day before International Human Rights Day, the police raided the high-rise office building where the church services were about to begin. They detained Wang Yi, his wife, and roughly a hundred church members. The officials also confiscated church property.

"Lord, help us to have the Christian's conscience and courage to resist this 'Orwellian nonsense' with more positive Gospel action and higher praise," read a church statement. "Without love there is no courage."

Jiang Rong and the others were released in the ensuing months, but in late December 2019, Wang Yi, in a closed-door trial, was found guilty of "inciting subversion of state power" and "illegal business activities" and sentenced to nine years in prison. About $7,200 of his assets were seized.

The US responded in a hurry.

"I am alarmed," Secretary of State Pompeo said. "Beijing must release him and end its intensifying repressing of Christians and members of all other religious groups."

★ ★ ★

I pray often for Wang Yi, who was nominated in 2025 for the Nobel Peace Prize by US Congressman Chris Smith and Senator Jeff Merkley—and he fully deserves it!

I am deeply concerned that the Chinese will not let him out of prison, and may not let him survive. They may view him as posing too much of a threat: a pastor with a moral authority that challenges that of Xi Jinping. If Xi were wise, he would release Wang Yi and embrace the changes he is calling for. I'm not holding my breath on that one.

Word is that Pastor Wang has lost a lot of weight, as he anticipated, and that he hasn't been allowed a Bible or a prayer book. Or, at least not on a regular basis, even a pen and paper. Yet I hear that he has written outlines of about a dozen future books and hymns.

In his head.

He is allowed to write one letter a month to his family, but it appears that, due to their religious content, they haven't been delivered. Similarly, it's uncertain whether the letters his family wrote to him were ever received.

I pray for Jiang Rong, as well.

Held in detention for six months after her husband was arrested, she is watched closely by security officials. I've been told she has suffered from depression due to isolation, and from high blood pressure.

I'm hoping that at least we can get their nineteen-year-old son, Wang Shuya, out of the country. As fast as possible. A lot could happen to Wang Yi's family as we approach the day he is supposed to be released, and most of it isn't good.

I've also thought about the transformation that Wang Yi made in the years prior to his arrest. He went from talking about "rights" to talking about the Kingdom of God.

That shift caught a lot of his supporters in China and abroad off guard. No pastor of a house church had been more political than Wang Yi.

Why the different approach?

Because he had come to realize that a regime change wouldn't change what is in people's hearts, where the true transformation must occur.

As he explained in *My Declaration of Faithful Disobedience*, "Changing social and political institutions is not the mission I have been called to, and it is not the goal for which God has given His people the Gospel." At the same time, and Wang Yi must have known this, he couldn't say the things he did—such as, "If Xi Jinping does not repent, he will perish!"—and *not* come across as being subversive. The CCP claims to be the answer to every aspect of life in China, and here comes a human rights lawyer-turned-pastor who rejects that notion in everything he writes and preaches. Of course he is going to be silenced.

Which makes his 2018 letter all the more poignant.

"The Bible teaches us that, in all matters relating to the gospel and human conscience, we must obey God and not men," he wrote. "For this reason, spiritual disobedience and bodily suffering are both ways we testify to another, eternal world and to another glorious King."

Every time I read Wang Yi's letter, I'm more certain than ever that the Kingdom of God will win out over the Kingdom of Man.

Because of people of faith such as Wang Yi who never stop believing. No matter what the CCP throws at them.

"For on earth," he wrote, "there has only ever been a thousand-year church. There has never been a thousand-year government. There is only eternal faith. There is no eternal power."

That makes me think of the Orthodox Church headquarters in Romania, which is in the same building the rubber-stamp legislature met in during the Communist era.

The Communists are gone and the Church now owns the building.

★ ★ ★

Wang Yi touches my soul in so many ways.

Not just because I pray for his future, but because being unable to talk to him, to hear his deepest thoughts and dreams, reminds me of the other men and women I can't talk to, who are imprisoned in China and around the world for daring to have a relationship with God and being unwilling to keep it hidden.

The names we don't know. The voices we don't hear. The brave individuals who, in all likelihood, will die behind bars.

I wonder: *What is on their mind as the weeks and months pass by? Do they question their faith, or is their faith stronger than ever?* I suspect the latter. Just as it was for Peter Xu. And, no doubt, many others.

I think back to when Sharon Payt came into my office and told me about the missionary in Uzbekistan who was in jail and the work we did to get him out—and more after him. The struggle for religious freedom has come a long way in these past three decades.

But not far enough. Not when people like Wang Yi languish in a prison cell.

For believing in his Lord and Savior. And in the eternal.

CHAPTER 5

I AM FROM HONG KONG

I THINK A LOT ABOUT the future.

About the young people who will pick up where these inspiring heroes—Peter Xu, Pastor Pan, and Wang Yi—leave off.

Which is why I was so heartened when I was introduced to Frances Hui in the fall of 2024. She represents the next generation of freedom fighters for Hong Kong and China. They are fearless, well-trained, and smart.

If only the CCP would be smart, as well.

If the Communists would just allow basic human rights, at least in Hong Kong—and I know I sound naïve—it would show the world that whatever China's ambitions might be, it is a government that lives up to its word. In this case, to the promises it made before taking control from the British in 1997.

Since September 2022, Frances, who is twenty-six years old, has served as the policy and advocacy coordinator for the Committee for Freedom in Hong Kong Foundation. She should be living in her native land, spending time with her friends and parents, and working as the journalist she set out to be. Instead, she is living in the United States. With a bounty of one million Hong Kong dollars on her head.

She has cared deeply about others for much of her young life. Thanks to the influence of her parents and her church.

Her parents didn't lecture her about the need to be there for her fellow man. They showed her. Day after day.

One of her father's heroes was John Melchior Bosco, known as Don Bosco, an Italian priest from the nineteenth century who founded the Salesians. There is a great deal to admire in the Salesians. They are always looking out for the poor. Don Bosco, who worked in the city of Turin and was devoted to the Virgin Mary, was especially concerned about the fate of juvenile delinquents and migrants who hung out in the streets.

Others thought that some form of punishment was the answer.

Not Don Bosco. He believed in love. He was eventually canonized by Pope Pius XI.

"My entire childhood was based around him," Frances said. "He was very different from other heroes. He was a model for me."

Instead of visiting their relatives and friends every Lunar New Year, as most people in Hong Kong did, Frances and her family celebrated the holiday with residents at senior homes. Her mom was a social worker.

Lunar New Year is about reunion with family. These were individuals who didn't have families to visit them.

"Not for praise or gain," she pointed out, "but simply because we all knew this world always needs more love and compassion."

Frances, unfortunately, had to leave her beloved Hong Kong when the authorities passed the National Security Law (NSL) in the summer of 2020, which essentially allowed the government to criminalize anyone it considered a threat. That included Frances. She had participated in the city's protests since her early teens, helping to coordinate rallies. Shortly after the act was passed, a friend with contacts high in the government warned her she was on the watch list and would likely be arrested.

Maybe. Maybe not. She wasn't about to take any chances.

In September 2021, less than a year after arriving in the United States, Frances became the first activist from Hong Kong to receive political asylum in America since the crack-down in 2019.[19]

She had mixed feelings about leaving. On the one hand, she was given a sanctuary where she could fight for the freedom of those she left behind.

On the other, it signified a final, painful break with living in the land she adored—a land she knows she may never see again.

"One hour before I left home for the airport," Frances said, she was "begging my parents to allow me to stay for a while longer, maybe a week."

Her parents knew better. She had to go, as harrowing as it was for everyone. Even one more week might have been too long.

On the flight to Seoul, Frances was in tears the whole way. From Seoul, she flew to Detroit and then to Boston.

Her parents had never been crazy about their little girl getting deeply involved in the protest movement. They worried about her grades and her safety. "At first," Frances told me, "they were proud that their kid was paying attention to society overall. But once I got really devoted, they got concerned."

Did their concern ever cause her to reconsider?

Nope.

"I've always been rebellious," she explained.

Having heard about the Tiananmen Square massacre her whole life, Frances realized early on how privileged she was to have been born in Hong Kong where there was freedom, unlike in China.

Then the freedoms became threatened. One at a time.

In 2014, inspired by the activist leader Joshua Wong, Frances, fifteen at the time, took part in the Umbrella Movement.

Why "Umbrella"?

Because that's what protestors used to ward off the pepper spray and tear gas the police fired to disperse the crowds.

They were demanding universal suffrage in the election of Hong Kong's chief executive, while the Chinese attempted to walk back from the constitutional promise to have the leader chosen by popular vote. At first the resistance was driven by students—Wong was eighteen—but it soon gained support from other segments of society. The protests went on for seventy-nine days.

Beijing's puppet government in Hong Kong held firm, abusing the protestors and ignoring the will of the people.

The movement died down. For the time being.

Frances, who had been out on the streets for almost all of the seventy-nine days, experienced a deep sense of loss.

"I wasn't sure where to go and what to do," she said. "I used to go to the site after school, and now that it was cleared, it became an ordinary highway again. I felt like I had lost a community where I felt a sense of belonging. I didn't know what Hong Kong meant to me until the Umbrella Movement. I saw the beauty of humanity. We all became neighbors even though they didn't know me and I didn't know them."

She didn't stay down for long. She couldn't afford the luxury. There were too many fights ahead.

Frances helped set up booths to keep spreading the message: We will not surrender. We will not let the CCP take our freedoms away.

It soon occurred to her that the best way to help the cause would be to become a journalist. And the best way to do that would be to study the craft in the United States. She attended Emerson College in Boston.

At Emerson she showed remarkable courage for someone of her age. For someone of any age.

One day in the spring of 2019, Frances got into a conversation with another passenger on a bus.

"Where are you from?" he asked.

"Hong Kong," she told him.

The passenger became incensed.

"You are Chinese," he said. "You need to fix your identity. You are from China."

Frances was now the one incensed.

She wrote an article for the student newspaper, *The Berkeley Beacon,* about what happened on the bus. Frances, an editor at the time, saw the op-ed as an opportunity to educate her American friends who kept telling her they knew little about her homeland.

In the article, "I am from Hong Kong, Not China," she got right to the point: "I am from a city owned by a country that I don't belong to."[20]

Frances explained how China, which was handed control of "the special administrative region"—that's how Hong Kong is described—by the British in 1997, had violated its pledge to allow "one country, two systems." She complained that during orientation at Emerson, her hometown was listed as Hong Kong, China.

"This move might flatter most of the Chinese students at Emerson," she wrote, "yet it upsets me to see how unaware the college is to this topic."

Frances was proud of what she wrote. Even after it turned her life upside down.

From then on, she felt that everyone was watching her as she walked around campus. She said she caught other Chinese students "whispering to each other" in the dining hall. *There she is, the girl who had the nerve to criticize China.*

That wasn't the worst of it.

The worst was when she saw a post on Facebook from a Chinese student: "Whomever opposed my greatest China, no matter how far they are, must be executed."

Frances, who was studying for finals, went into a panic when she saw the post, crying the whole night. She was used to seeing hateful words on Facebook. This post was different. She knew who the student was. They had mutual friends.

She went to the school authorities, who did absolutely nothing. I'm not shocked. That's how much a large part of higher education in this country has lost its way. It fails over and over to call out evil for what it is. And here is the scariest part: I'm not sure the people running some of these schools know what evil is anymore. We saw how morally deficient they are from their response to the antisemitism on their campuses that emerged after the Hamas attack against Israel on October 7, 2023.

According to Frances, instead of censuring the Facebook post, the school put out some mealy-mouthed statement asking both sides to respect each other. Give me a break. The post had called for Frances to be executed. As she pointed out, "You certainly shouldn't stand for students who make threatening statements and hateful comments."[21]

It comes down to the obscene amount of money that the Chinese Communist Party pours into our universities. Let me repeat: our universities. I saw it in Kansas when I was the governor. Schools throughout the United States are heavily dependent on students from China who pay full tuition. The money has bought a lot of things, one of the worst being silence. Frances told me that when she met with the director of international student affairs at Emerson, the woman talked about how hurt the Chinese students had been after reading her opinion piece.

Are you kidding me? What about Frances? She was the one whose life was being threatened.

I asked whether she has ever regretted writing the article.

Not for one second.

From then on, her self-confidence went way up. She began to help mobilize the Hong Kong diaspora around the world to show its support.

In November 2019, Frances headed back to Hong Kong for two weeks to vote in a district council election. She had never voted before.

With the pro-democracy protests still going on, she took on a bigger role than ever.

At first, she reported on the protests but then ...

"I would be standing in the crowds, thinking, *I want to be part of this*," she said. "There were times I actually took off the press ID."

Frances didn't realize it at the time, but her days on the sidelines were over. Probably for good.

She went to Boston and was set to graduate in May 2020 but left for Hong Kong again in March just before Covid shut everything down.

A few months later, the National Security Law was passed.

It was the latest blow in a year marked by one attack on democracy in Hong Kong after another, starting when the authorities proposed the Fugitive Offenders and Mutual Legal Assistance in Criminal Matters Legislation (Amendment) Bill, which would have allowed Hong Kong citizens to be extradited to mainland China to receive "justice" at the hands of the Communist Party. Mass protests broke out as people realized that their last legal protections—and the last vestiges of independence from the Chinese regime—were about to be stripped away.

Listening to Frances, I couldn't help thinking of the trip I made to Hong Kong in March 2019 when I was the religious freedom ambassador. The main purpose was to give a speech to the Foreign Correspondents Club.

I had given speeches before in Hong Kong. Once, when I was a member of the Senate, I called for direct elections of the mayor instead of Beijing appointing the chief executive, which would demonstrate a true two-systems approach between Hong Kong and the mainland. And I urged that a free market and the rule of law would better serve the people of Hong Kong.

Beijing called me a pig. I felt honored. I had struck a nerve, which meant I was doing something right.

I struck that nerve again in 2019.

The speech was cleared by the appropriate channels in DC, but while I was jogging in front of the Capitol on the night before I left for Hong Kong, something hit me that I hadn't put in the text: "China is at war with faith. It is a war they will not win."

That's what politicians refer to as *the money line*—the line the press would jump all over.

Except there was a problem.

Because the line hadn't been cleared by the State Department, I would be taking a risk. I included the line in my speech anyway, and it had the desired effect.

"You could feel the air go out of the room when you said that," a friend told me.

It came, however, at a cost. That night, I was set to meet with about thirty people from all walks of life in Hong Kong.

Only two showed up.

I was saddened but not surprised.

Many of those who didn't come maintained strong business connections to China. One wrong word or appearance with the wrong person—yours truly—and those connections would have dried up in a nanosecond.

I wondered whether I would still have a job when I returned to Washington. I didn't know if I was in the clear until I showed up for work the next day and there weren't any beefy security guys waiting to escort me from the premises. Better yet, one of Secretary of State Pompeo's top assistants told me that the "speech was one of the most important ones of the whole administration."

It was an honor to work in the first Trump administration, but it was also liberating to become a private citizen again in early 2021.

I didn't have to clear what I said with anyone. I could let the Lord be my guide.

Which is exactly what Frances Hui has done. Time and time again.

★ ★ ★

It pains me greatly to see what has happened to Hong Kong. What was once a proud, honorable city looking toward the rest of the world is now focused on its precarious relationship to mainland China.

From 2020 to 2022, roughly a half million people, many of them young professionals like Frances Hui, left Hong Kong for other opportunities in the UK, Canada, Australia, and the United States. In their place, the Chinese implemented a program, the Top Talent Press Scheme, to import men and women from the mainland who had been raised (brainwashed) in the dogma of the CCP. This was right out of their playbook: Switch out a troublesome independent population for one molded by the government.

They are doing it in Hong Kong—and, as we shall see, in Tibet and Xinjiang. Taiwan will be next if Beijing ever assumes control. We can't let that happen.

We won't let that happen.

Hong Kong used to be full of hope. Now it is full of fear.

That includes the churches. While many remain open, the sermons aren't what they were before. Not even close. One Protestant pastor was reportedly sentenced to thirteen months in prison for sedition.

"Priests have to be very careful about what they say," Frances told me. "They don't talk about political issues."

She said there was an invisible threat to religion in Hong Kong.

"It is hard to tell people that religion is under siege because no churches are being demolished, unlike in China," Frances said.

In a report she compiled in 2024, entitled *Hostile Takeover: The CCP and Hong Kong's Religious Communities,* here is what Frances discovered:

- Since 2021, the Catholic Diocese of Hong Kong has conducted at least three seminars on Sinicization of religion with the state-controlled church and has ordered clerics, seminarians, and religious sisters in Hong Kong to visit Beijing.
- The religious textbooks are filled with prayers embracing China and Chinese identity (translation: the CCP).
- The national flag symbolizing atheism must be displayed in faith-based schools next to sacred symbols.
- Religious groups and leaders are co-opted to promote patriotic and socialist ideology.

The Church was an ally for protestors during the Umbrella Movement. Not anymore.

"It used to be a haven for when any of us were attacked by police and needed first-aid help," Frances said. "The priests conducted masses on the streets. Now, I can't even name them."

Another glaring example of Chinese oppression in Hong Kong is what has happened to the well-known publisher Jimmy Lai, and Cardinal Joseph Zen.

I will start with Lai, who, as expected, was found guilty by a panel of three judges—no jury—in December 2025 of two counts of conspiracy to collude with foreign forces and one count of conspiracy to publish seditious material.

Two months later, he was sentenced to 20 years in prison. A death sentence.

Lai, in his late seventies, didn't commit any crimes. In 2020, he took part in the pro-democracy protests—which, of course, as China sees the world, *is* a crime.

As for Cardinal Zen, who attended Lai's sentencing, he was arrested in 2022 for failing to register a charitable fund.

The cardinal, now in his nineties, possesses a great deal of moral authority. Far more than Xi Jinping. And power in someone else's hands, especially anyone from the clergy, is something the CCP will simply not tolerate.

Cardinal Zen was a fierce critic of the Vatican's secret deal with China. (I'll tell you more about that in the next chapter, when you'll meet Nina Shea, a valiant advocate for persecuted Catholics.) As the cardinal put it, "A church enslaved by the government is no real Catholic Church." He was also a staunch participant in the Umbrella Movement and one of the first to speak out against the proposed extradition law.

I asked Nina if there was a chance of talking to him.

"It would be dangerous," she told me. "Granting an interview for this book could be a crime under the National Security Law. The risk isn't only to him but to the Hong Kong Church."

I pray Cardinal Zen will call on the people of China to "Be not afraid."

I'm sure he has no concern for his own life. His focus is in keeping the churches and schools open and operating. A government-run Catholic school is not a Catholic school.

I have met Cardinal Zen several times and know his strength, courage, and boldness. He is not a "tree that bends before the wind blows," as the Chinese saying goes.

Here's what he said to explain why he has been so outspoken all these years:

"I speak out because I am the voice of the voiceless."

His voice is needed more than ever.

★ ★ ★

As for the bounty (one million Hong Kong dollars; more than $128,000 US) on her head, it was issued in December 2023 by the Hong Kong police, who claimed that Frances violated the National Security Law by "colluding" with foreigners. The Chinese-controlled authorities called her an "absconder" and revoked her passport. Adding insult to injury, they accused her of "inciting secession." Bottom line: Hong Kong citizens who make efforts to preserve their independence are accused of "seceding" from the mainland.

In April 2025, a few days before Easter, I caught up again with Frances on a Zoom call.

She looked awful, and it was no wonder why. About a week earlier, her parents had been picked up by the police for questioning. It was the second time this had happened. The first time was shortly after the arrest warrant and the bounty was put on her head. That was to be expected. This time, Frances was shocked.

The only explanation she could think of was that the government was retaliating for sanctions the US had imposed against Chinese and Hong Kong officials, something she had long advocated for.

Frances spent days in her DC apartment watching press footage of her parents. Leaving the police station, her mom frowned behind her mask while her dad shielded his eyes as he walked through a crowd of reporters. "It broke my heart," she wrote to friends and colleagues, "to see them treated as though they had done something wrong when they hadn't. They are good people. Good citizens who care for others. They are just a mother and a father, like anyone else's."

She was overcome with guilt. Her parents were going through this because of her.

She felt like she had failed them.

"As a daughter," Frances told me, "my duty is to take care of them as they age and give them a sense of relief that I'm taking care of myself. I've been unable to do that. I'm adding to their burdens."

I tried to talk her out of blaming herself, to get her to see that she has not failed as a daughter. Being a parent, I have no doubt they are proud of her standing up for her ideals and for her people.

It hurts me to see what the whole ordeal has done to her health, physically and mentally.

She told me about the painful boils on her skin that come out of nowhere every two or three months. And about the nightmares she's been having…for who knows how long. The details differ each time, but they always involve her being back in Hong Kong. "Scared I would be found out," was how she put it. "That they arrested me and tackled me."

Frances hasn't spoken to her parents, both in their sixties, since December 2023. That was her idea.

Not wanting to assume any additional risks, she told them she wouldn't call any more. They understood. She last saw them when they came to the United States in 2022. I wasn't surprised to hear she steered clear of any conversations about her work.

If they were to be questioned again by the police, Frances said, "they can just say that they don't know anything. What is important for them to know is that I built a life here, that I am safe."

Whenever her parents want to get a message to her, they do it through intermediaries.

After they were detained and questioned last April, her father sent a message to her through those other channels: "Tell Frances to stop doing what she is doing. She should stay low and keep quiet."

That's not going to happen, and her parents know it.

Frances hasn't shared much about her parents since she left Hong Kong, and she feels that has been a big loss.

"This is what authoritarianism does," she explained. "It strips away your power and your freedom—to think, to speak, to express yourself. It makes you feel powerless in every part of your life. Eventually, it tries to erase the parts of you that define who you are."

Shortly after her parents were released, she posted on social media for the first time "about who they are to me, and how they made me who I am.… It means a great deal to reclaim the narrative and those memories—to stand up for them." By writing about them, she has pointed out, "I challenged the Chinese regime for its treatment of innocent citizens. Because this is how I want my parents to be remembered—not as the people in those videos being chased like suspects, but as who they truly are."

What about the bounty? I asked.

"It's ridiculous," she said. "They can't arrest me here. It's just a threat to intimidate us."

She was prepared for the bounty—Frances wasn't the first in Hong Kong to be targeted—but once issued, it was "surreal to be one of the names listed and see my face on the screen." And to hear from friends who noticed her picture in the streets, at a police station, or at the airport.

Yet she kept doing her work, and that's another thing I admire about Frances Hui.

"We won't let the government think they are getting to us," she said.

★ ★ ★

Every modern movement that has had any measure of success against oppression—the anti-human trafficking movement, the Save Darfur campaign, the Invisible Children movement to prevent the abduction of children to use as soldiers in Central Africa, and so forth—it occurred to me, has been energized by youth and its willingness to take risks. In a way, and I mean no disrespect, you could say that young people don't know any better. They see a wrong and stand up to it. Unlike those whose heart might be in the right place but are afraid of what they might lose if they were to speak out.

I ran that point by Frances. She understood.

"We said all the time during the Umbrella Movement (in 2014) and the pro-democracy movement that the future belongs to the young people."

She hears a lot of regret from older generations: "It's because we didn't fight when we were younger that you have to suffer now."

"I don't want us to have the same regrets," Frances said.

CHAPTER 6

THE ADVOCATE

NINA SHEA GREW UP IN Yardley, Pennsylvania, a small, sleepy town founded in 1682 by a Quaker in search of religious freedom, close to where General George Washington crossed the Delaware River in December 1776 to wage the Battle of Trenton, catching the British by surprise and turning the tide in the Revolutionary War.

"My father was the dentist in town," Nina said.

The only dentist?

"There might have been one more."

The cause of religious freedom needs advocates like Nina Shea. People who prefer telling the facts over being diplomatic. No matter where the trail may lead.

For Nina, the trail hasn't been what she anticipated. After attending Smith College, a highly regarded all-women's college in Northampton, Massachusetts, in the mid-1970s, she went to law school in Washington, DC, and expected to work for one of the top corporations. Those were the jobs that everyone pursued out of law school. The jobs that paid the big bucks.

She got one, all right. But she was miserable.

"I felt like I was renting out my brain," Nina said. "There was nothing interesting about drafting energy regulations for oil firms."

She switched to criminal defense work. Same result.

One day, after interviewing a client, she noticed her purse was missing. She can laugh about it now.

In addition, a great deal of the progress in protecting the constitutional rights of the accused had already been accomplished by that point.

Nina, inspired by Jimmy Carter (and later, Ronald Reagan), was looking for an area of law where she could make a difference. That area turned out to be human rights.

Which fulfilled another deep desire of hers. Nina yearned to see more of the world. Those ambitions were first fueled by the stories her parents shared, by the toy dolls they brought home after trips overseas, and by the summer after her sophomore year of high school that she spent studying Renaissance art in Florence.

Her first big break came in the mid-1980s when she was in her twenties and working for the International League for Human Rights in New York, which was accredited by the United Nations. While she was helping to prepare the case for the Human Rights Commission in Geneva on behalf of Andrei Sakharov, the brilliant Nobel Peace Prize-winning Soviet physicist-turned-dissident, her boss became ill.

"Nina," the boss told her, "you will have to go to Geneva instead of me."

She wound up helping the Sakharov family draft speeches and introducing them to reporters and diplomats. Sakharov had been exiled to Gorky due to his persistence in documenting Soviet repression, and at that time had been forcibly hospitalized.

"He stood by his principles," Nina said, "knowing it would result in being stripped of the privileges he had as the top scientist in the country. The Soviets took away his freedom and the research he had been working on for years."

Later on, thanks to perestroika, she met the great man, who was then an opposition member of parliament, at an event in DC.

"I went over and shook his hand and he thanked me for my work," she recalled. "I was thrilled."

Was she nervous?

"No. I wasn't having a physics discussion with him," Nina quipped.

Working on Sakharov's case, she got her first inkling that her efforts, as well-intentioned as they might be, wouldn't please everyone in the diplomatic community. A delegate to the U.N. from France berated her: "Don't you understand that you are poisoning the atmosphere of the United Nations?"

Nina didn't back down. She explained that working for Sakharov was a matter of human rights, not Cold War posturing. Besides, the Soviet Union had infiltrated every level of the U.N. bureaucracy.

"It's already poisoned," she told the French delegate.

She had found her calling.

"I felt like there was a need for my voice and [the voices of] others who were working on it," she said.

Nina soon turned her attention to Central America. "I went with a group of doctors from Colombia University looking into the cases of their colleagues who had disappeared because they treated the wrong person, maybe a person connected to the leftist insurgency—and when people disappeared back then, they were killed by right-wing death squads."

She helped lead a human rights investigation in Nicaragua, which was controlled by the Sandinista Marxists. Nicaragua and El Salvador were mirror images of each other.

On Nicaragua, Nina went her own way when her former colleagues on El Salvador objected to her reports criticizing the

Sandinistas' persecution of the Catholic Church and other human rights violations.

"The Sandinistas were ... attacking the Catholic Church, shutting down the independent press, and taking over the lands of the poor farmers," Nina recalled, "so I wrote about that. First, they said, 'You got duped, you don't know what you are talking about.' Then, 'You got to stop doing it, you don't know the whole story. You're helping Reagan.'"

She didn't stop, needless to say. And she found others to work with.

Nina has been making contacts in all corners of the globe ever since—coalitions of dedicated, devout leaders, both priests and leaders of civil society, who understand and support repressed communities. This was, she said, "after the Cold War, when there was a dearth of reporting on human rights and little interest anywhere on matters of religious persecution." In repressive regimes, she explained, religious minorities and disfavored religious communities—no matter the particular faith—"are typically the first to be attacked and last to remain standing. Their members are among the only ones willing to die for their beliefs. They are by definition truth seekers."

The first human rights leader to inspire her was Humberto Belli, the Nicaraguan writer and devout Catholic who ran the editorial page of the pro-democracy newspaper *La Prensa*. He had been a member of the Sandinistas in the early days but broke away once he understood the implications of their Marxism.

In the 1990s, Nina worked at Freedom House, a nonprofit in Washington, DC, promoting democracy and human rights, taking on one cause after another.

One of her causes that has impressed me deeply was her campaign in the aftermath of 9/11—the majority of those attacking America that day were Saudis—to revise textbooks in Saudi Arabia that encouraged violence toward Jews, Christians, and some Muslim sects. In one textbook it was written that Israel had been "established on the land of Palestine wrongfully and in transgression," and asserted that the "whole [Muslim] nation lives in a Jihad against international Zionism manifested by the State of Jewish gangs." Another passage taught teenage boys that violent jihad is the "pinnacle" of Islam. The textbooks were required in every Saudi school and exported around the world.

Nina's fight against the textbooks got her in trouble, a situation she would often find herself in. I get the sense that a part of her relished it, that it proved she was onto something.

"I left Freedom House under pressure from the board of directors," she told me, "because I was reporting very critically on the textbooks. The US State Department was aghast that I had done that, that I had risked our oil relationship with [the Saudis], and complained to Freedom House."

The textbooks were cleaned up. Though it took a lot longer than it should have.

In 2017, Nina testified before a House committee.

"Since 9/11," she said, "the State Department has barely raised the issue and at times has even worked to cover up their toxic content. It has not held the Saudi government to its repeated promises to the United States to reform its textbooks."

By that point, Nina was spending more of her time working on religious freedom in China. She had started down that path in the late 1980s, when she noticed how many people working in Washington were focusing on the persecution in East Germany and Poland and Czechoslovakia while ignoring the oppression in "this other communist country, this gigantic place...China."

★ ★ ★

In her first report on China, for the Puebla Institute, which she helped found (it would later be renamed the Hudson Institute's Center for Religious Freedom), Nina wrote about Catholic bishops and priests and Protestant pastors who were in prison.

There would be more reports to come.

Her most recent one, which she compiled for the Hudson Institute, came out in October 2024.

It was vintage Nina. No holds barred.

The report is critical of the Chinese Communist Party for its ongoing imprisonment of bishops without due process and finds fault with the Vatican, as well.

"In over 30 years of dialogue with China," Nina wrote, "the Vatican has kept silent or publicly downplayed China's denials of religious freedom." (She pointed out that, in contrast to Vatican diplomats, Pope John Paul II and Pope Benedict XVI acknowledged the persecution.)

I met with Nina the day before the report was released, and she was even more emphatic in person.

God bless her.

"It is worse than silence," she said, referring to the Vatican diplomats. "It is kowtowing."

She decided, however, to avoid any direct criticism of the late Pope Francis.

"The China policy preexisted him," she pointed out. "It was driven by others in the Vatican bureaucracy. He was a busy man, relying on them." In the early '90s, when she wrote about the bishops and priests who had been incarcerated by Mao and were still in captivity two decades after his death, Monsignor Claudio Maria Celli, a diplomat who is still a top negotiator with China for the Vatican, told Nina she was hurting the Church—by which he meant the Church's dialogue with China.

Nina didn't believe she was hurting the Church—she was certain her approach was consistent with Pope John Paul's approach to the Soviet Union—but was concerned enough that she reached out to several Catholic friends who were close to the pontiff.

"If this is true, I will stop working on it," she told them.

One of the friends put her in touch with Cardinal John O'Connor, the Archbishop of New York.

O'Connor went right to the top.

"In my presence, he called Pope John Paul," Nina recalled.

Tell her not to stop, the pope, or an associate speaking for him, told the cardinal.

That was all she needed to know.

"I felt like I had been rescued," she said. "I was redeemed. My reputation and my work had been on the line."

Soon afterward, she had another conversation with the Monsignor.

"Are you telling me that, as a layperson, I have to follow your diplomatic strategy?" she asked.

"Of course not," he responded. "You have the right, as a layperson, to do whatever you want in that regard."

That doesn't mean the Vatican's China team has been eager to give her any assistance over the years. Quite the contrary.

Nina shared an email she received in 2020 from a top Vatican adviser on China in response to her request for a list of bishops in captivity. He told her he preferred to promote dialogue over confrontation. "For reasons of my own attitude and approach to the situation in China," he wrote, "even if I had the list you look for, I would not share it, as you will understand."

When I read the email, I was beside myself. I have always been in favor of diplomacy, of searching for common ground, in even the most unlikely places—I was a member of the Senate when compromise was not a dirty word—but to withhold the names of those heroes from a human rights activist like Nina Shea is not justified under any circumstance. People in this country and around the world, and not just Catholics, must know who they are and what has happened to them.

As for the precious dialogue with China, where, exactly, has that gotten us?

The bishops are still in prison, and the genocides against the Uyghurs and the Tibetan Buddhists and Falun Gong haven't abated one bit.

How ironic that the Catholic Church, the institution that should be backing Nina Shea the most, is the one that has thwarted her.

Nina, as you might expect, wasn't deterred. Then or ever since.

"I feel bound to tell the facts and let them fall where they may," she told me. "Even if it is hopeless, and at times it does feel like that. And even if there are voices who criticize me. I'm not a Vatican diplomat, and I wasn't trying to be liked by those who were standing with the oppressors."

She backed off a bit in the late 1990s when things opened up to some degree. "A lot of bishops on my early list," she said, "were let out."

Still, she remained wary of China's true intentions. She "was reading everything and talking to everyone."

She was particularly disturbed by the US government's willingness to grant Most Favored Nation Status to China and to overlook credible reports of atrocities such as the mounting disappearance of prisoners of conscience, the forced organ harvesting, the forced abortions in pursuit of the one-child policy, and the torture of individuals of all religions.

In her 2024 report, she identified ten Vatican-approved bishops who have been detained off and on for years...some for decades. That's not counting those who died, or for whom there is insufficient information to know their fates.

The ten bishops have strongly opposed joining the Chinese Patriotic Catholic Association (CPCA), which is part of the United Front of the CCP and requires that its members pledge to be independent of all foreign influence, including the pope. Which begs the question: If a Catholic bishop is independent of the pope, whom does he answer to?

A secret deal China signed with Rome in 2018, which was renewed by Pope Francis in 2024 for another four years, has been used by the CCP to pressure Catholic clergy to join the association. And has allowed the Chinese to fill leadership positions in the Catholic dioceses with priests who have joined the CPCA; in other words, the government effectively picks the bishops.

As Nina explained in her report, "It is evident that the CCP aims to suppress all religions, including Christianity, and replace them with the dogma, values, and images of the party."

The best known of the ten is Cardinal Zen of Hong Kong, whom I told you about in the chapter on Frances Hui. But all their stories are very much worth telling. Let me give you brief profiles of two others:

BISHOP JAMES SU

Bishop Su, from the Hebei Province, has reportedly been in captivity since 1997, although we can't be certain he's still alive. He was incarcerated, as well, in the '50s, '60s, '70s, and '80s. The authorities once refused the bishop medical care after a wheelbarrow of rocks fell on him and broke both legs. I'm very touched by what he said decades ago at an underground Mass: "If I have to go to back to prison, that's where my people are."

BISHOP JOSEPH XING

Bishop Xing, from Shanghai, the most populous Chinese diocese, has been missing since 2011. Sadly, the Vatican has given its support to Bishop Joseph Shen Bin, the head of the CPCA, who was transferred from the city of Haimen to take over in Shanghai. In a 2022 interview, Bishop Shen said "we must adhere ... to the "direction of the Sinicization of the Catholic Church in China."

I read Nina's report with much dismay—even more so, I confess, because I hadn't known about the ten bishops.

And I'm supposed to be an expert in religious freedom.

I'm far from alone. "Nobody knows about them," Nina said.

In addition to blaming the Vatican, she said the media is part of the conspiracy of silence.

"They should be investigating this and reporting on this," she said, but "they take their agenda from politicians who, while interested in trade and the fentanyl crisis, are not paying attention to religious freedom." That's a tragedy, because as Nina points out, "If the media were reporting on it, the heads of churches would feel more pressure to talk about it and the government would follow."

Why, one might wonder, aren't we familiar with the names of the dissidents in China, as we were with the dissidents in the Soviet Union during the 1970s and '80s?

Well, as Deep Throat (FBI Deputy Director Mark Felt), the famous Watergate source, told *Washington Post* reporter

Bob Woodward in the movie, *All the President's Men,* "Follow the money."

Back then, nobody in America bought goods from the Soviet Union. Now, everybody buys goods from China.

Nina's criticism of Vatican policy toward China puts me in a difficult position.

I have deep admiration for the men of the cloth and the vows of celibacy they have taken. I am in awe of their commitment and sacrifice. On the other hand, the Vatican is not infallible when it comes to geopolitics. We should listen with respect to its position on foreign policy, but we don't have to follow it. It could be misguided. I'm not criticizing Rome on its interpretation of the Bible. I'm criticizing Rome for being silent about a regime that is committing three genocides.

Some have compared the Vatican's silence toward the atrocities in China with Pope Pius XII's failure to criticize the Nazis during the Holocaust. It's a fair comparison.

I think back to the role Pope John Paul II played in the breakup of the Soviet Union. We need another John Paul. If we were to have an alignment between Rome and the United States on China, similar to the common cause we had in the 1980s against the Soviet Union, we could move Heaven and Earth.

Whether Pope Leo XIV will be another John Paul remains to be seen.

In 2019, Secretary of State Pompeo and I met in Rome with Cardinal Pietro Parolin, the Vatican's top diplomat, and Archbishop Paul Gallagher, the secretary for relations with states. Both of us were extremely critical of the China deal.

"You don't negotiate with evil," I told Gallagher off to the side. "You throw it out."

I felt a bit uneasy, a layman arguing with an archbishop about evil, but I couldn't let the opportunity slip away. Too much is at stake.

It didn't seem to make a difference. Gallagher didn't respond.

In 2018, before the Vatican entered into the agreement with China on the appointment of bishops, I asked Nancy Pelosi to let Rome know she was opposed to the proposal. The messenger is often as important—sometimes more important—than the message itself. I figured that perhaps Pelosi, a liberal Democrat, might receive a better hearing with a liberal-leaning Vatican than I could as a conservative Republican. She reached out but got nowhere.

★ ★ ★

After Nina's report came out in 2024, she didn't hear a word from the Vatican.

Which was no surprise.

"I didn't expect them to break the deal because of my report," she told me. "But I was hoping that the Vatican would succeed in getting a bishop released by now, given all the concessions it has made to the CCP. One of the bishops has been in prison twice this year [2025] so far, and the year isn't over, and has been detained eight times without due process since the deal was signed. He never knows when they are going to come knocking and take him away."

No wonder she is so frustrated. Nina has spent over thirty years trying to make the world aware of what China is doing to these bishops and often feels she has too little to show for it. Some of these bishops—they were priests at the time—were in the first report she wrote in the mid-1990s.

She tries her best not to feel discouraged. Perspective helps.

"I keep thinking of the shepherds of the Church who are alone and isolated and can't fulfill their ministries," she said. "Can you imagine their lives? They are not in touch with their church, their families, with anybody. So who am I to complain?"

Two things keep her going. One is the realization that change, as hopeless as it might seem, is possible. She points to the collapse of the Soviet Union.

"Nobody expected that until it happened," she said. "Nobody. And not a shot was fired."

The other is the relationships she has established with church leaders and laymen in South America, Africa, Asia, and so forth, who are on the front lines resisting the campaigns against Christians. "The unsung heroes of the persecution," she calls them, who "go through incredible fear and pain to do what they do." Such as the late Cardinal Ignatius Kung of Shanghai. "I was awed by his fortitude and faithfulness. He had spent thirty-three years in Chinese prisons and labor camps."

Working with these heroes, she said, "is inspirational and makes me feel like I should be doing more. I could make a difference if only I worked a little harder."

If anything, she is more energized than ever.

"Before," she said, "it was admiration for those people who would stand up, the Sakharovs of the world, and the pastors. But I also now see another dimension, which is American security. If China wins, America won't simply be a second-rate power. We will become slaves. If we lose to Beijing, it will be the end of the world as we know it."

I couldn't agree more.

Nina is worried about the future of Catholicism in China, and I share her concern.

"Without the underground church," she said, "you can't perpetuate the Church. Some say in a hundred years that China will still be a Catholic country, but how do you get to a hundred years if you can't educate children in the faith? You can't even educate them in some semblance of faith." Since 2018, she went on, "the Chinese regime has ensured that the Patriotic Catholic bishops do not allow children into their churches. Who will be the next generation of priests and pastors?"

To put it in more theological terms, the future Catholic Church in China may not be the Church of Rome. It could become the Church of Xi Jinping.

I asked Nina what steps she would recommend to free the millions under Chinese tyranny.

For starters, she said, a speech from President Trump.

I pray for that speech.

Donald Trump is the first president since Dwight D. Eisenhower to stand up to China. He is in a position to call out China on religious freedom the way Reagan called out the Soviet Union on human rights.

Nina also believes the State Department should ask to meet with the bishops who are in detention. I have no illusion China would agree to such a meeting, but at the very least, the request must be made. Sooner than later. Nina is 100 percent right, as well, about the need for the secretary of state to bring up the imprisoned bishops, the Uyghurs, Falun Gong, Tibet, and so forth, in every bilateral meeting with China.

This is a national security issue as well as a moral one. Will the United States of America, as it celebrates its 250th birthday, stand up for religious freedom in China and around the world?

Our allies in China are the people of faith. And China obviously considers its war on faith a matter of national security. So why can't the US—the entire West for that matter—do the same?

★ ★ ★

Nina Shea is many things. Diplomat is not one of them.

She told me she needs to be "less nuanced" when it comes to China in the years ahead.

Is she kidding? Less nuanced? How is that possible? What would that even mean?

"It means," she explained, "to really lay blame on particular voices who have been silent, or even worse, covering up. That is the way to build pressure. It means having accurate analysis based on all the facts, even the inconvenient ones."

In the spring of 2025, I had lunch in a Washington, DC, suburb with Mihrigul Tursun, a survivor of China's genocide against the Uyghurs. I have never met anyone with more courage than Mihrigul, whose son was killed by the Chinese. Photo courtesy of Michael Arkush.

No one has been a stronger advocate for religious freedom than former Congressman Frank Wolf, pictured here with the Dalai Lama. It still amazes me how Frank pulled off a secret trip to Tibet in 1997—a trip that certainly had its share of scary moments. Photo courtesy of Frank Wolf.

Enes Freedom, a former player in the NBA, has sacrificed so much to stand up for what he believes in. He will be an important voice for years to come and, hopefully, a member of Congress one day. Photo courtesy of Michael Arkush.

Arjia Rinpoche, a high lama in Tibet, was eight years old when his life changed forever in 1958. He tried to work within the system in China, but had no choice but to escape in the late 1990s and seek sanctuary in the United States. Photo courtesy of Arjia Rinpoche.

God bless Nina Shea, a senior fellow at the Hudson Institute in DC. She is committed to her Catholic faith but also committed to telling the truth when it comes to the Vatican policy toward China. Photo courtesy of Nina Shea.

Pastor Pan, a modern-day Moses, led members of his Mayflower Church from China to South Korea to Thailand to, finally, Midland, Texas. It is a remarkable story. It should be made into a movie. Photo courtesy of Michael Arkush.

Peter Xu, an early leader of the House Church movement and considered the Billy Graham of China, was first imprisoned under Mao in the 1960s. In his mid-eighties, now living in Colorado, he remains a strong advocate for religious freedom. Photo courtesy of Michael Arkush.

Frances Hui planned to be a journalist. But due to the Chinese attacks on democracy in her native Hong Kong, she turned into an activist. It led to her leaving home and getting political asylum in America. Living in DC, she continues the fight. Photo courtesy of Frances Hui.

I often pray for Pastor Wang Yi, who has been imprisoned in China since 2018. I met him briefly in 2006 when, as a human rights lawyer, he came to Washington to meet with President George W. Bush. I yearn to see Wang Yi in good health and back with his family and mission. Photo courtesy of ChinaAid.

Wang Chunyan, a follower of Falun Gong, spent seven years in prison for refuting lies spread by the Chinese Communist Party. She also lost her husband. Yet nothing will deter her from spreading the truth about the practice that saved her life. Photo courtesy of Wang Chunyan.

Part Two

THE WAR ON TIBET

CHAPTER 7

FREE, BUT NOT HOME

IT IS IMPOSSIBLE TO IMAGINE what the eighth Arjia Rinpoche felt when the only world he had ever known came to an end.

He was eight years old.

The signs, more ominous with each passing day, had been building for months: daily study groups that focused on "democratic reform" (translation: reeducation in the ideology of the CCP and allegiance to Mao Zedong) and went on for hours and hours.

Religious training coming to a sudden halt.

Strangers in blue uniforms taking away prized possessions from the storeroom. He would find out later they were from the "Confiscation Bureau."

Arjia was the high lama of the historic Kumbum Monastery in the Qinghai Province in northern Tibet.

Tibet had been functionally independent until its takeover by the Chinese Communists in 1951. The Tibetan people differ in ethnicity and religion from the Chinese. The CCP has savagely persecuted the Tibetan Buddhists, particularly the monks, who play such a pivotal role in religious matters. A unique feature of Tibetan Buddhism is its belief that key figures—including the Dalai Lama and leaders of monasteries—are reincarnated when they die and that they can be identified as children.

Arjia was discovered in 1952, when he was only a toddler, after a long search for the reincarnation of the monastery's beloved spiritual leader.

From that time on, he and his two older brothers lived at the monastery, where he learned to be a Buddhist monk. That was his life leading up to October 15, 1958—the day everything came crashing down.

Arjia stood by helplessly as Chinese soldiers arrested about five hundred monks. Many were shoved onto trucks and taken to prison, never to be seen again.

He was too young to understand. He was not too young to be terrified.

"In that first wave of arrests," he wrote in his 2010 memoir, *Surviving the Dragon,* (the dragon being the Chinese oppressor) "my entire household was taken from me, leaving me completely alone for the first time in my life.... I had no idea who was going to take care of me, or what I should do."[22]

Arjia's story is different from some of the other accounts in this book. He was never a bold crusader for democracy and human rights. He was subjected to Communist "reeducation" from childhood and forced to endure humiliation after humiliation for decades in order to help his people, and simply to survive. And he finally found the courage to break free.

★ ★ ★

What Arjia and the monks had to endure on that October day and in the days to follow was so horrific I hardly know where to begin.

Along with nearly a hundred other children, many of whom had been in training to be monks, he was taught to eavesdrop on others and report anything suspicious. He was also told to keep an eye out for hiding places where any of the monks might have stored objects that hadn't yet been confiscated. Most degrading of all, he learned how to denounce those who were labeled as counterrevolutionaries in line with the Great Leap Forward, the CCP's campaign to switch from an agrarian to industrialized society.

All this, again, at eight years old.

Arjia thought it was a game at first, as he practiced what he was learning with one of his new teachers.

Some game.

When it became his turn to do it for real, Arjia denounced a highly respected monk by the name of Gegue Gendan Sopa.

"I stepped up to the podium dutifully," Arjia wrote, "and recited such slogans as 'Leniency to those who confess their crimes, and severity to those who refuse.' In my ignorance, I spat on him."[23]

In 2025, I interviewed Arjia, now in his mid-seventies, on several occasions.

I asked about the incident. He told me he had no choice. Which doesn't make what he did less awful. Or the guilt less severe.

"That began a new era," he said, "where bad things started happening to me."

Arjia was far from alone.

Monks, no longer allowed to wear their precious robes, were forced into the fields for slave labor. The Chinese set up loudspeakers on the mountainside near the monastery to broadcast Communist propaganda.

Arjia and the others were hungry. All the time.

The Great Leap Forward, which lasted until 1962, caused the worst famine in history, with some estimates as high as forty-five million deaths.

"Our soup became thinner and thinner," he wrote. "Now it consisted of wild vegetation, a few potatoes, and almost no flour.

All of us had terrible diarrhea, and some of the monks' faces had turned a sickly green. Other monks were becoming too weak to walk."[24]

Arjia knew better than to complain. Thin soup was better than no soup at all.

The Kumbum Monastery, like countless others in Tibet, would never be the same. It had housed four thousand monks. Now only a few hundred were left.

One day, some people Arjia had never seen showed up to work in the fields and be reeducated in the "socialist academy." Word was that they were high lamas, former government officials, and intellectuals.

"Sometimes they did participate in sessions on Marxism and Leninism," he wrote, "but the only academy graduation I ever saw was death from starvation. Eventually the task of disposing of the dead became so overwhelming that their bodies were thrown into ditches on the temple grounds. On our way to and from school, we children learned to avert our eyes from this terrible sight, and to hurry past."[25]

★ ★ ★

Arjia's story began with a mystical quest for a great Soul to help his people.

The quest for the eighth Arjia Rinpoche started, as is traditional, about a year after the passing of the previous one, with a search party from the monastery that roamed the countryside to gather facts, impressions.

Signs.

The search party eventually narrowed its choice to ten boys who stood out for their extraordinary intelligence, a recollection of events or places they had never been to, or an unusual skill in music or another pastime that was a favorite of the lama who had passed.

They took their time. A second year went by. This was an important matter. They needed to get it right.

The selection ceremony occurred in the monastery—on the spot where Lama Tsongkhapa, the founder of the Gelug school, the largest branch of Tibetan Buddhism, was born in 1357.

How the current Arjia Rinpoche—his original name was Yung Drung Dorje—the ninth of eleven children, got the nod is a story that needs to be told.

The Panchen Lama, the second most well-known Tibetan religious leader, held a goblet containing ten tsampa balls (dough made of water, barley flour, and butter) each with the name of a finalist written on a strip of paper inside. (The Panchen Lama had seen the future Arjia Rinpoche's name earlier and pointed to it, declaring, "Yes, this is the one," but the boy's instructor, who also happened to be his uncle, was concerned about nepotism. A fascinating process, if you ask me).

Anyway, after the Panchen Lama swirled the balls around a few times, one ball jumped out. The piece of paper it contained read: Yung Drung Dorje.

Before long, the new, eighth Arjia Rinpoche was taken, along with his family, to the Kumbum Monastery.

His new home. His new life.

His older brothers, Nori and Chibo, were allowed to stay with him for the next six years, but his parents hung around for just a few months. How difficult it must have been to say goodbye to their son, but what an honor it was for them and the entire family. From then on, Arjia's parents would see him at least twice a year. He had two families now. The one he was born into, and the one he had joined.

With the best tutors, Arjia learned his prayers, although he was never great at memorizing, and got to know the rich customs of the Tibetan Buddhist monastery. There was a lot to take in. Yet he was still a boy, so there was plenty of time to play, as well. Visitors often brought him toys.

Life was good. Until that October day in 1958.

Over the next decade, he would try his best to live according to dharma, the philosophy of the Buddha.

The Chinese didn't make it easy for him.

During the Cultural Revolution, he was forced to denounce, among others, the Panchen Lama himself, who, branded as a counterrevolutionary, was imprisoned and tortured. In 1962, the Panchen Lama had written a document known as the *70,000 Character Petition*, which he presented to the Chinese government. He criticized Communist China's actions in Tibet going back to the 1950s.

The monks who refused to denounce him were sent to prison camps. Some were murdered.

Arjia told me that denouncing the Panchen Lama, who taught him about wisdom, was more difficult than it would have been to denounce his own parents.

As ashamed as he was, Arjia kept his feelings to himself. Trusting the wrong person could be fatal.

A visit to Dolun, where his family lived, was also very painful.

So much had changed in the eight years since he had moved to the monastery. His mother's face, he wrote, was "a study in sorrow," while his younger sister and brother stared at him "without saying a word."[26] His family assumed at first that he was a member of the Red Guards, the gang that had recently taken

Pema, Arjia's older brother, to a class-struggle meeting. Only after Pema came home safe and sound did everyone accept Arjia. His family shared heartbreaking stories. His father, Baldan, had been arrested in 1959 and never returned. Later, a man arrived with a letter about a deceased prisoner who matched Baldan's description. How he died, Arjia has no idea.

The Red Guards could have shown up again at any moment. So Arjia soon went back to the monastery, where he worked ten hours a day without a break. Year after year.

In September 1976, working on a construction project with other Tibetan Buddhist monks, he heard the announcement over the loudspeaker that Mao had passed away.

One monk couldn't contain himself. He was so happy, he began to sing.

Arjia, on the other hand, searched deep into his soul and found compassion for Mao.

Remarkable, really, when you think about it. In his position, most people would have found nothing but rage.

Mao is right up there with Adolf Hitler and Joseph Stalin as one of the most sadistic figures of the twentieth century. Of any century. In fact, he is responsible for killing millions more innocent people than either one of them. Arjia—like others of his faith, a strong believer in karma—would later write: "Now it was Chairman Mao's turn to fear what was coming to him in his next life."[27]

With Mao's passing, and the arrival of Deng Xiaoping, there was hope in China.

For a decade or so. Until Tiananmen Square.

During the Deng Xiaoping regime, Arjia got along fairly well with the Chinese Communists, taking a job in the government in order to advocate for his people in Tibet and for other religious communities. Still, no matter what he told himself, he couldn't help wondering whether he was betraying his heritage.

In the mid-1980s, an official from the Ministry of Public Security by the name of Comrade Ho asked Arjia to join the CCP. That put him in quite a bind. If he said yes, he would be aligning himself with the party that had been responsible for momentous death and destruction. If he said no, he would be assuming a tremendous risk. The party didn't take rejection very well.

Arjia said no, declining to give a reason.

Fortunately, Comrade Ho didn't press the matter. If he had, who knows how it would have ended.

On January 28, 1989, Arjia heard over the loudspeaker of another death.

This one was much different from the first.

The Panchen Lama was dead, from an apparent heart attack. He was only fifty years old.

Unlike the Dalai Lama, the Panchen Lama had remained in Tibet and suffered the consequences. He had been released from prison in 1977 but was under house arrest until 1982.

In early 1989, he again criticized the Communist regime, in a speech he delivered in Tibet.

Five days later, he was gone.

Many don't believe he died of a heart attack. It was widely speculated that he was poisoned.

I asked Arjia, who had seen the Panchen Lama only a few days before he died, what he thought.

"He was very happy," he told me, "and then all of a sudden he died. That doesn't make sense to me."

The search for the next Panchen Lama, the eleventh, took a long time, as usual. Finally, on May 14, 1995, the Dalai Lama chose Gedhun Choekyi Nyima, a six-year-old from Lhari County in Tibet. Three days later, the new Panchen Lama was kidnapped by the CCP. Shocking, isn't it? He hasn't been seen since. The Chinese say they have kept him and his family away from the public for their own protection.

Another lie. The next time they tell the truth will be the first time.

In November of the same year, the Chinese government chose its own Panchen Lama—the false Panchen Lama, as most outside the grasp of the CCP would refer to him.

Yet Arjia, who sat in on many meetings during the selection process, was obligated to bow to him.

"I felt soiled by the gesture," he wrote, "but once again no one dared to defy our government handlers."[28]

As the years rolled on, Arjia, who went on his share of foreign trips, thought about defecting.

What stopped him was knowing he was needed back home—he had returned to the Kumbum Monastery, serving as director—and that if he were to bolt, others in the group he travelled with might be in danger.

★ ★ ★

Last July I reached out to people I know in the Tibetan community.

"How bad is the situation these days?" I asked. "And what can the United States do about it?"

Pretty bad, they told me.

The citizens of Tibet are under constant surveillance—cameras in the monasteries and listening devices in their homes. The mass surveillance technology was introduced in Tibet in 2012 by Chen Quanguo, who would later bring Big Brother to the Uyghurs in Xinjiang.

The Tibetan people can't trust anyone. Their monasteries are filled with Communist Party *cadres,* placed there as spies. Tibetans face dire consequences if they are even found with a picture of the Dalai Lama.

Even more frightening is what's happening with the children.

The future.

The Chinese have forced parents to send their young ones to preschools and boarding schools where they are taught Mandarin Chinese and indoctrinated in party propaganda. This is the cultural genocide of Tibet.

"We have reports," said Lobsang Sangay, a former president of the Tibetan government in exile, who now teaches at Harvard, "that after two months at boarding school, children come back home and look at their grandparents with disdain and say, 'Because of you, we are not making progress. You are too religious, too conservative. We should modernize, be more Chinese and less Tibetan.'"

The Chinese are also forcing monasteries to translate ancient Buddhist texts into Mandarin.

"Some might write off the project...as nothing more than an experiment," Dhondup T. Rekjong, a Tibetan scholar, wrote, "but looking at the history of the Communist Party's most repressive and damaging policies and regulations, they often begin as seemingly innocuous 'experiments.'"[29]

Still, I am deeply moved by the resilience of the Tibetan people.

The selection of the next Dalai Lama will be a huge test for them, and for the world. It must be conducted by the Tibetan Buddhists in their traditional manner. The Dalai Lama, on the eve of his ninetieth birthday last July, made that abundantly clear. The hypocrisy of the CCP never ceases to astound me: an officially atheist organization claiming the right to appoint the next spiritual leader of Tibetan Buddhism.

Once the CCP rolls out its false Dalai Lama, the Tibetan people will reject him soundly.

Just as they have rejected the false Panchen Lama the party anointed in 1995.

The Chinese claim that many from all over the mainland travel great distances to be in the presence of the Panchen Lama. Truth is, they come because they are paid to come and might be in trouble if they don't; in one instance, I was told, they walked as slowly as possible to make certain they didn't arrive in time. The false Panchen Lama has made only a couple of trips away from China. He isn't accepted by the Tibetan diaspora around the world.

What also gives me hope is how the Tibetans, against all odds, and against one wave of oppression after another, remain standing. Faithful. Defiant. Following the customs and beliefs they have followed forever.

"This is our tradition," said Tencho Gyatso, the president of the International Campaign for Tibet, based in Washington, DC. "We've done this from generation to generation. This is the fourteenth incarnation of the Dalai Lama. It's a system we've grown up with and is part of our beliefs. This bond will continue to the fifteenth."

★ ★ ★

In 1998, the eighth Arjia Rinpoche knew it was time to leave China. For good.

On the same ground where he denounced his fellow monks forty years before, Arjia was forced to denounce His Holiness, the Dalai Lama.

Arjia knew the CCP was planning to have him tutor the false Panchen Lama. In addition to the humiliation, the pressure would have been like nothing he had ever encountered.

From the age of eight, Arjia almost always went along with the Communists.

Not anymore.

In his mid-forties, he was ready to take the biggest risk of his life. If he were to fail, he would end up in prison. Or worse.

He didn't have much time. The party was about to appoint him to be a member of the National Committee of Chinese People's Political Consultative Conference and chairman of the Buddhist Association of China. He would be constantly in the company of others. There would be no way he could escape.

But two questions needed to be addressed before he put any plan into motion.

Where would he go? And who would he take with him?

His first thought, naturally, was India, where the Dalai Lama lives in exile. Except to get there, he would have to travel with his large entourage through Tibet, which is under the control of China. (The Chinese refer to the area as the "Tibet Autonomous Region," refusing even to call it "Tibet.")

Anyone in the entourage could be a spy.

Fortunately, a student he trusted suggested that Arjia could get a friend in Guatemala to invite him for a visit. With an invitation in hand, he would be extended an entry visa to that country.

Mission accomplished.

As for who would accompany him, he decided on his thirteen-year-old nephew, Chenlie Rejie, his personal attendant, his bodyguard, and the bodyguard's wife. They would fly on KLM from Beijing to Guatemala, pretending to be a tour group.

But there was a problem: Their tickets were on standby. Anything could happen.

And nearly did.

At the airport Arjia spotted someone he knew from the State Administration for Religious Affairs.

"I immediately turned away from him," he wrote, "and folded up my collar to avoid being seen. Luckily I did not have my robes on, and I had grown a mustache, so he did not recognize me."[30]

It looked like they were in the clear. Though his heart raced when the customs officer checked everyone's passport.

"He glanced at each one," Arjia wrote, but "without much interest. Whether it was the blessings of the Dharma Protectors or the officer's negligence, our passports were finally stamped and we boarded the plane just minutes before takeoff."[31]

Arjia didn't relax until the plane took off.

But he wasn't home free even then.

In Guatemala, after examining their passports, a military official, surrounded by armed soldiers and a German Shepherd, said the whole group might have to be sent back to China.

The minutes felt like hours.

Finally, the official returned with the passports and said they were free to go. It turned out that Arjia's Guatemalan friend had done what is customary in these situations.

He bribed the soldiers.

★ ★ ★

Arjia and I chatted again in the summer of 2025, shortly before the Dalai Lama's birthday. He had hoped to go to India for the big day, but the doctors advised against it. He wasn't feeling his best.

I have met the Dalai Lama on several occasions. Once, when I was the ambassador-at-large for international religious freedom, I traveled to Dharamshala to make emphatically clear the US government position that any future Dalai Lama must be selected by the Tibetan Buddhist community, not the Chinese government.

The line of those seeking the Dalai Lama's counsel was always long, and yet he took his time with every person. I recall him once rolling two balls in his hands. I asked our host what he was doing. "Divination," he told me.

What Tencho Gyatso from the International Campaign for Tibet told me about His Holiness is so true. "The connection that this Dalai Lama, in particular, has with the Tibetan people," she said, "is beyond what those of us who live in the free world can imagine.... He touched so many hearts. Why? Because he represented truth and justice."

The last time I met with him was in June 2019. He was as tranquil as ever but also firm. As he should be.

"I will outlive the Communists," he vowed. "I may live to one hundred twenty years old."

As for Arjia, after a few months in Guatemala, he moved to the United States. He met in New York with the Dalai Lama, who asked him to keep a low profile. His Holiness was attempting to open up negotiations with Beijing and didn't want anything to get in the way.

Arjia did what His Holiness asked. That doesn't mean it was easy.

"A lot of things happened in China," he told me, "and I wanted to come out and clarify everything."

Finally, after about two years—the negotiations weren't making progress, and the Dalai Lama no longer had any problem with Arjia speaking out—he got his chance, telling his story before a committee in Los Angeles that was looking into religious freedom in Tibet.

He has been telling his story ever since.

In 2005, he became director of the Tibetan Mongolian Buddhist Cultural Center in Bloomington, Indiana. He later started a Tibetan Center for Compassion and Wisdom in Northern California.

During our last interview, Arjia told me about the dreams he had almost every night after leaving China.

In one, the police bring him back to China and put him in prison.

In another, he is at the airport when he realizes he doesn't have a passport.

He also had a dream in which he couldn't summon the courage to leave.

The four others who escaped with him to Guatemala had similar dreams.

Arjia spoke to Tibetan Buddhist teachers, who suggested he try more meditation. They also reminded him that he was in the United States. That he was free.

The nightmares eventually went away.

Yet as comfortable as Arija is in America, it can never be home.

"I enjoy democracy and freedom of speech and freedom of religion," he told me. "But I'm still a Tibetan. I want to go back, and I can't."

Arjia is worried that Tibet as we know it will disappear. At times, he has blamed the horrible things that have happened to his people on karma. Thinking that they must have done something wrong in their past and the bad karma was bound to catch up to them.

With all due respect, I disagree. It isn't bad karma that killed the monks and destroyed the monasteries. And forced an eight-year-old boy to denounce those he held dear.

It's the Chinese government. And the evil that is Communism.

One thing the US government could do is back the Dalai Lama's Middle-Way Approach of true autonomy for Tibet within China. Where the Tibetans run Tibet, not the Chinese. The secretary of state or the vice president should meet with the Dalai Lama and publicly endorse his approach. If the CCP won't go along, we should call for the complete independence of Tibet and back this internationally.

I often think of something the Tibetans believe in with every part of their being: *anicca*, the doctrine of impermanence. That if they remain patient, everything will work out.

I sometimes struggle with the concept, looking for policy changes that might make a difference today. Not decades, or centuries, from now.

Yet this is who they are and how they have endured. Against one of the mightiest forces on earth.

Who I am to question them?

"Never lose hope, however dark the sky may become," the Dalai Lama wrote in his 2025 book, *Voice for the Voiceless.* "As our saying goes, 'If you fall nine times, you get up nine times. Always remember that a bright sun awaits behind the clouds.'"[32]

CHAPTER 8

THE PIONEER

I HAVE LONG CONSIDERED FRANK Wolf, a Congressman who represented the Tenth District in Northern Virginia from 1981 through 2015, the pioneer in the fight for religious freedom.

There has been no one like him.

Frank got Congress to pass the International Religious Freedom Act in 1998 (it was later named for him). That was no easy task. The members of the foreign policy establishment, Democrat and Republican, have never been crazy about religious freedom. They think it distracts from developing sound foreign policy and creates unnecessary conflicts. In addition, they believe getting the federal government involved in religious disputes violates the separation of church and state. That's simply not true. The United States, the beacon of freedom since its founding—slavery being the exception—has a moral obligation to do whatever it can to stand up for the human rights of every individual on this planet, and central to those rights is religious freedom.

The first time I heard Frank give a speech was shortly after I joined the House of Representatives in 1995. He was addressing the Republican Caucus, the GOP being the majority party in the House for the first time since the first Eisenhower administration in 1953.

That's a long time to be out of power.

Whenever a speaker came to meet with us, inspiring my colleagues and I to keep fighting for the legislation we were certain would change the world, the scene reminded me of a pep rally before a high school football game.

That wasn't the feeling when we heard Frank Wolf.

Frank brought up a host of issues he cared deeply about, don't get me wrong, but more importantly, he reminded members that no matter how much we might accomplish, we must never forget about our families.

Never.

Too bad I didn't follow his advice. Frank's speech came a few months before my wife warned me I was losing touch with our children. And before I was diagnosed with cancer.

Frank Wolf possessed moral authority, something that wasn't true about every person I worked with in Congress. On both sides of the aisle.

Over the years, I went to his office on numerous occasions seeking guidance.

What committees should I serve on?

What foreign policy objectives should I focus on?

How can we get certain human rights legislation passed?

Frank made a ton of superb suggestions, one being that I switch from the Foreign Relations Committee to the Appropriations Committee. I resisted for the longest time, convinced Appropriations was filled with big spenders and I was a balanced-budget guy. Frank helped me realize the obvious: Most legislation that is passed by Congress is attached to an Appropriations bill. You need to be on the committee that handles the money.

Each time I left his office, I felt invigorated, ready to do the people's work.

In 2004, Frank and I were the first members of Congress to visit Sudan during the genocide against Darfur. Villages were being systematically destroyed, residents forced into mass refugee camps in which there was no escape from rape, pillaging, cholera and dysentery. And death.

Working with him closely, I couldn't have been more impressed.

Not by his intelligence. That, I already knew.

By his compassion for the persecuted and helpless.

★ ★ ★

There's a reason Frank Wolf is so empathetic. He knows what suffering is all about.

He stuttered terribly as a kid, and it's still noticeable in his mid-eighties. There are words he can't get out of his mouth, so instead he searches for substitutes. In Congress, his colleagues told stories when they hung out in the cloakroom. Not Frank. He would have been embarrassed if he were to mess up a word, and he'd been embarrassed enough already.

When he was growing up on the south side of Philadelphia, boys being boys, the others made fun of him. He never started fights, but he never backed down from them, either. Come to think of it, I haven't seen him back down from any challenge, personally or professionally.

"The abuse was a good thing," he said. "It toughened me up."

Years later, he and his wife, Carolyn, went to see the movie *The King's Speech,* in which King George VI (the father of Queen Elizabeth II), played by the wonderful actor Colin Firth, fights valiantly to overcome his stuttering. Walking out of the theater, "I was crying," Frank told me. "Weeping. Bawling. My wife was with me. People couldn't understand what was going on."

Frank was no scholar in high school, and that's being kind. In a graduating class of 190 students, he finished 176th. No wonder he didn't think college was in his future.

He worked as a mail boy with the Curtis Publishing Company—it put out *The Saturday Evening Post*—which was across the street from Independence Hall. Frank spent a lot of time at Independence Hall and other landmarks, learning about history—he read every biography he could get his hands on—and dreaming about the day he would be part of it. He often touched the Liberty Bell, which wasn't in a glass case back then. How fitting. Securing liberty, in America and abroad, has been his mission for decades.

"In third grade, we had to take a test," he said, "of what you want to be when you grow up. The first thing I put down was a pro football player for the Eagles. A congressman was the second thing. People laughed at me."

Frank had hoped to go to Penn State but wasn't accepted. Not with his grades. The University of Mississippi accepted him, however, and Frank started in the fall of 1957. Oxford, Mississippi, felt like a whole new world to someone from South Philly.

The folks down South were very friendly, Frank said, but he was still so lonely that one day he scanned through the yearbook to see if there was anyone else from Philadelphia.

There sure was.

From Philadelphia, Mississippi.

Fortunately, after a year, his grades were good enough for Penn State to accept him, and that's where he met Carolyn Stover at a popular student center called the Hub. Frank didn't look his best that night. There were bandages on his face from a fight the night before.

The fight had come about because someone had made fun of his stuttering. The guy beat him up pretty badly, with Frank ending up in the infirmary.

Even so, Carolyn saw the man beyond the bandages, and they were married only two weeks after her graduation, much to her father's displeasure. Not exactly the biggest believer in Frank's future prospects, he wanted the couple to wait until Frank finished law school and his military service.

Frank, as you can tell by now, isn't the waiting type.

Georgetown Law School was next.

He lasted one semester. Law was boring, filled with a bunch of documents and contracts. Human beings, that's what fascinated Frank Wolf. Then and for the rest of his life.

He took a job in construction—at the Rayburn House Office Building, of all places. Next was the Blount Construction Company, where he worked on the entrance ramp to the Teddy Roosevelt Bridge.

Then at the Smithsonian.

"My job," he wrote in his 2011 memoir, *Prisoner of Conscience*, "was cleaning the antique weapons up in the tower. The museum smelled revoltingly of the dead rats that had crawled behind the walls after ingesting a fatal dose of rat poison."[33]

He lasted less than two weeks.

From there, he landed a position with the State Department, but after assigned to the passport division, which was located in the basement, he quit.

On the first day. Before lunch.

Do we notice a pattern here?

With nothing else on the horizon, it seemed as good a time as any to take another crack at law school.

Or not.

Moments after walking into the admissions office at Georgetown, he walked out. Without saying a word. He enlisted in the Army instead. This was only a month after the Cuban Missile

Crisis gripped the nation in the fall of 1962. He ended up serving at Fort Knox in Kentucky and Fort Gordon in Augusta, Georgia.

He felt an obligation to his country. Obligations mean a lot to Frank Wolf.

Only the military wasn't the answer, either.

Back to law school he went. Law school, at least, would be the means to the position he had craved since he was in elementary school and realized he would never make it with the Eagles: a seat in Congress.

Taking classes, boring or not, at night—he worked during the day, representing the National Canners Association on Capitol Hill—he made it through Georgetown Law in 1965. Three years later, when Frank was still with the Canners, his boss asked him to fill in for him at a fundraiser for Richard Schweiker, a candidate for the Senate. Schweiker would later be chosen by Ronald Reagan as his running mate prior to the Republican convention in 1976. They would have formed quite a ticket...if the party hadn't nominated President Gerald Ford.

During the fundraiser, Frank got into a conversation with Congressman Pete Biester Jr. from Pennsylvania.

Frank was critical of a vote Biester had cast, though he doesn't remember which one. There have been a lot of votes since then.

Biester appreciated the fact that Frank was challenging him. During the first time they met. Only Frank.

Before the evening was out, Biester offered him a job as a legislative assistant. Frank said no. He liked his boss at the National Canners Association. He'd had his shares of bosses he didn't like.

A few weeks later, Frank changed his mind.

Watching Bobby Kennedy's funeral at St. Patrick's Cathedral in New York, he was deeply moved by Ted Kennedy's eulogy, in which he referred to the line his brother often recited, which had originated with the famous playwright George Bernard Shaw:

"Some men see things as they are and say, 'Why?' I dream things that never were and ask, 'Why not?'"

Frank realized he was an idealist, and public service was his calling.

Some may think it's strange that it was something a Democrat said—a Kennedy, no less—that inspired Frank. I don't. The two parties may have disagreed on the issues, sometimes vehemently, but in the end that's what used to bring out the best in Washington politicians, Red and Blue: Passion. Commitment. Integrity.

Frank had it all.

In 1976, at the age of thirty-six, he ran for Congress. His district encompassed Arlington and Fairfax, Virginia, both suburbs of Washington, DC.

He got creamed.

Two years later, he ran again. And lost again.

He figured his career was over.

"Nobody runs a third time," said Frank, who was resigned to a future in law.

Except Frank Wolf.

He was encouraged by Michigan Congressman Guy Vander Jagt, head of the National Republican Congressional Committee, who sent him a note: "You did a great job. I hope you'll run again."

In giving it a third try, he took quite a risk, a risk that, as much as I have loved public service, I can't imagine I would have taken in a million years. And if that crazy notion had entered my mind, even for an instant, Mary Brownback would have set me straight. Frank cashed in all of his insurance policies and took money out of his retirement account. God Bless Carolyn. I don't know any other spouse who would have gone along.

"You could say it was irresponsible," Frank admitted. "I had five children."

He ran like it was the last race of his life, and that was to his advantage. Every day, he hopped on the Metro, the DC railway network, and jumped from car to car. He also got a list of all the supermarkets in his district, going to each one three or four times. Thursdays and Fridays from 3:00 to 7:00 p.m. were particularly busy times, as were Saturday mornings from 8:00 to 11:00. "I'd go to the right, which was usually the produce section," he said. "I'd go up and down a few times and then say goodbye to people as they left, giving them my brochure. I never went anywhere without my brochure."

He also walked into different offices in the district, taking the elevator to the top floor and working his way down. You might get arrested if you tried to do that today.

Frank operated under what he called the four *S*'s.

Smile.

See. (He looked everyone in the eye.)

Shake. (He shook every hand.)

Sale. ("I appreciate your support," he said at the end of each conversation.)

Even so, in late August 1980, his pollster, a good friend of Ronald Reagan's, gave him the bad news:

"You're down twenty points."

Frank was not deterred. Not one bit. He asked his pollster to see if Reagan, who was in a tight battle with President Jimmy Carter—Reagan didn't pull away until near the end—would send a letter endorsing Frank. He certainly would.

Day by day, Frank gained more and more momentum.

"The last week before the election," he recalled, "there was a parade in Vienna [a Virginia suburb of DC], and for the first time I could feel people cheering for me. I knew I had a chance."

Wolf defeated the incumbent, Representative Joseph L. Fisher, a liberal Democrat, 51–49 percent.

The life he had been dreaming about since he was a boy was finally his.

★ ★ ★

In his first two terms, Frank focused on mass transit and roads—the widening of Interstate 66 was a big issue for his constituents, and so was improving the safety at National Airport (now Ronald Reagan Washington National Airport)—as well as a range of issues affecting federal employees, his district including the most of any in the country.

In 1984, he got a call from Congressman Tony Hall of Ohio.

Frank and Hall, who is a Democrat, didn't agree on policy matters, but they were good friends. And still good friends today.

That's another thing I admire about him. Instead of seeing members of the other party as opponents, if not enemies, Frank—perhaps taking a cue from the relationship President Reagan fostered with Tip O'Neil, the Speaker of the House—saw them as potential allies. Observing that kind of cooperation stuck with me. I worked on the first anti-human trafficking bill with Senator Paul Wellstone from Minnesota. No one in Congress was more liberal than Wellstone. I also worked with Ted Kennedy on a Down Syndrome bill. I wish there were more politicians these days who looked for such opportunities.

Frank Wolf and Tony Hall, along with Dan Coats from Indiana and Bob McEwen from Ohio, met for lunch every Tuesday. They talked about the events of the previous week but not about politics. They prayed and then ate, and I can tell you from my own experience that when you pray and eat with someone, you have a chance to touch each other's soul.

So many in Congress—and I was guilty of that early in my career—focus on gaining power and rationalize it by saying that it's better for the constituents they represent.

That may very well be true. But that's not how Frank operated.

His authority didn't come from assembling a power structure. His authority came from his faith and trustworthiness.

"Have you been seeing what's going on in Ethiopia?" Hall asked him that day in 1984, referring to the famine in that country from which hundreds of thousands would eventually die.

"You ought to go."

Frank, who had been out of the United States only once his whole life—and that was to give a speech in Calgary—went, all right. The trip, traveling with members of World Vision International, a humanitarian aid group, changed his life.

People were dying all around him.

It is one thing to be aware of a famine. Another to be there in person.

"Congressmen have to see and feel and touch and taste," Frank explained.

A year later, Hall took him to Romania, where Frank witnessed more oppression. Nicolae Ceaușescu, the nation's last Communist leader—he wouldn't be ousted until 1989—was destroying churches and committing countless other atrocities.

In 1991, Frank went to China. He and Congressman Chris Smith, another great champion of human rights, met with the premier, Li Peng, and brought up the country's human rights violations, which the Chinese strongly denied. That did not stop Frank. He took a list he and Smith had compiled of nearly eighty Christians who had been arrested and tried and handed it to the premier. Li Peng wouldn't touch it, so Frank—he said the idea was spontaneous—placed it on an end table near him.

Looking back, he told me it was a stupid move, that the security officials protecting Li Peng could have tackled him, and the optics would have been horrible.

I don't agree. It wasn't stupid in the least. It was the right thing to do.

Frank visited a prison factory in China where roughly forty inmates were making socks. Some of the prisoners had been involved in the demonstrations at Tiananmen Square. He asked for a pair of socks, and the warden obliged. Frank, who still has the socks, lent them to Senator Daniel Patrick Moynihan, who held them up while delivering a speech on the floor about China's oppression.

Which leads us to Frank's 1997 trip to Tibet.

Tibet had been on his mind for quite some time. The year before, he had helped Congress pass three measures related to human rights, including one on Tibet. But as with Ethiopia and Romania, he needed to see the situation for himself.

Only, how?

The Chinese weren't keen on letting members of Congress visit Tibet. They knew they had something to hide. A lot to hide. And given they were aware of Frank's record on China—he hadn't wasted any opportunity to criticize the CCP—he would have been the last person to be granted a visa.

Which left only one solution. He would have to sneak in.

With help from the DC-based International Campaign for Tibet, Frank obtained a visa by pretending to be part of a trekking group. On the application form, he listed his profession as lawyer. Which was, technically, true.

He was taking another risk that I can't imagine I ever would have taken. Or anyone else in Congress, for that matter. Frank Wolf was the closest thing we had to Indiana Jones. If the Chinese had discovered his identity when he was in Tibet, he could have been detained, or worse. I would put nothing past them.

In any case, he made great use of his time on the ground.

Frank was only the second sitting member of the House of Representatives to visit Tibet since the Chinese crushed the Tibetan uprising and the Dalai Lama fled to India in 1959. Accompanied by Charlie White, a member of his staff, and aided by a guide and interpreter, Daja Wangchuk Meston, the son of Americans who had gone to Nepal and India in the 1960s, and been raised in a Buddhist monastery, Frank asked questions. Tons of them. He wanted to hear the truth, as disturbing as it might be.

The Tibetans wanted the truth to get out, as well. Their lives depended on it. Their country depended on it.

One woman, with tears in her eyes, appealed to him: "Please tell President Clinton to help us. When the United States speaks out and puts pressure on the Chinese government, things get better. Prisoners get released. But when the United States is silent, as it is now, things get worse."[34]

I wish I had been there. I would have assured the woman that if there is anything in life I was sure of, it was that Frank Wolf would not be silent.

One day, a taxi driver took Frank and Daja to the Drapchi Prison. Frank was worried the driver was putting himself in danger.

The driver didn't care. What he cared about was the prisoners—and the chance to get word about their condition out to the world.

"Prisoners are routinely beaten and kicked and poked with electric sticks," the driver told Frank.[35] "Political prisoners are isolated from the general population and kept in unlighted and unheated areas with no sanitary or medical facilities and almost no food or water."

Frank went to the Jokhang Temple, the holiest site in Tibet, and visited monasteries in Lhasa. "All monks are afraid," one monk said. "We are not allowed to practice our religion and the people are suffering greatly." (Even possessing a picture of the Dalai Lama, you might recall, could be dangerous, though it didn't deter Tibetans from showing Frank a handheld photo before quickly putting it away.)[36]

He realized Tibet was in danger of no longer being Tibet. The number of Chinese in Lhasa was nearly twice the number of Tibetans.

Frank couldn't wait to return to the US to share his observations with Congress and the American people.

Easier said than done.

After landing at Kathmandu in Nepal, where the parents of a former staff member were to pick up Frank and the others, the plane took off again without unloading its passengers.

Back to Tibet.

Frank and Charlie were taken to a hotel in the middle of nowhere. They walked to the airport nearby in search of a phone—they weren't allowed to use one at the hotel—to alert the people waiting for them in Kathmandu of what had gone on. Unsuccessful, they went back to the hotel, and this time they weren't allowed to leave. Consider it a form of house arrest.

What a terrible night that was. With all the walking back and forth to the airport, and running out of water at one point, Frank got very sick.

He felt like he was going to die.

The next morning, the Chinese put them on a bus to the airport. Officials took forever to look over his passport. How they never discovered he was a member of Congress still seems hard to believe. They wouldn't make that mistake today.

They finally let him go. Frank was never so relieved in his whole life to be in the air, and Lord knows he made a lot of trips over the years.

They passed Mount Everest and made it to Kathmandu, then to India and, at last, home sweet home. As brave as Frank is, he recited more than his share of prayers along the route.

Before leaving Kathmandu, Frank warned Daja, the interpreter, that he would in danger.

Especially once Frank's findings became public.

"Daja," he said, "do not go back. Do...not...go...back."

Unfortunately, Daja did go back to China a few years later, where he was captured. And perhaps tortured. While being held captive, he jumped out of a window. Or was pushed. We'll never know. He got out of China, eventually, and made his way to the US, but in the summer of 2010, Daja died in Boston.

I never met Daja, but he was a hero. Like Frank, he did everything he could to get the word out about the persecution in Tibet.

Soon after arriving in DC, Frank gave a press conference. He didn't mince words.

"I want the world to know what is going on in Tibet," he said. "When people know, they will demand that China change its policy of bootheel subjugation and end what one monk I met termed 'cultural genocide.'... The clock is ticking for Tibet. If nothing is done, a country, its people, religion, and culture will continue to grow fainter and fainter and could one day disappear."

The Chinese called Frank "a slanderer." Big surprise. The irony is beyond belief. And once they discovered where Frank and the others had been staying, they closed the place.

The situation in Tibet today, as I described earlier, is more depressing than ever. Even so, much of the world remains silent.

Not Frank Wolf.

When I met with him two years ago in DC, he was as passionate on the subject as ever.

His goal is to stop the lobbying that goes on in support of China. I agree with him 100 percent. Some of the most prestigious law firms in Washington work for China.

The same China that is committing three genocides.

As Frank put it, "Would you have allowed someone to lobby for the Nazis?"

Peter Schweizer of the Government Accountability Institute reported in 2022 that twenty-three former members of Congress, from both houses and both parties, have lobbied for the People's Republic of China or for companies linked to its military and intelligence services.

We need a total ban. Because here's what will happen if we don't pass one:

The CCP will continue to hire lobbyists, who will continue to co-opt congressional staff, members of Congress themselves, and the think tanks that greatly influence the making of public policy. These hired guns will gain information and help shape US policy toward China in a way favorable to Beijing. While many former officeholders will turn down the big money, many will accept, convincing themselves they are advancing the cause of peace and understanding between the two superpowers.

The Apostle Paul once wrote to his understudy Timothy that "the love of money is a root of all sorts of evil, and some by longing for it have wandered away from the faith and pierced themselves with many sorrows."[37]

Frank Wolf has no staff. No travel budget.

Only Frank and Carolyn standing up for one oppressed group after another.

In 2024, he and I spoke at a rally in DC to draw attention to the crisis in Sudan. Almost no one from the press was there, and only a few members of the public.

At eighty-seven, he is still a voice for the voiceless.

He reminds me of Johnny Cash, who kept singing till the end.

★ ★ ★

Sometimes when I think of Frank, my mind drifts to a gathering in 2019, when I was the religious freedom ambassador.

We held an event at the State Department, and I asked Frank to speak about the persecution in China. Of course he would. Better yet, he made a suggestion that very few, if any, members of my party would have made: "You should put Nancy Pelosi in there, too."

Keep in mind that Pelosi was the last person the Trump administration would have wanted to be part of any program I was assembling.

But Frank didn't care about the optics. He cared about making the strongest possible statement about Chinese atrocities, and Pelosi was committed to the same objective.

The two went on the stage and received a standing ovation. I couldn't have been more proud.

I once asked Frank if feeling the pain of others so deeply has ever been a burden. The answer was yes.

Even so, the boy from South Philly wouldn't have it any other way.

Part Three

THE WAR ON FALUN GONG

CHAPTER 9

TELLING THE TRUTH

SO MUCH IN THIS BOOK is about loss.

Seventy-year-old Wang Chunyan, whom I met in the spring of 2025, is another example.

Chunyan has suffered one loss after another—the greatest loss the love of her life, her husband Yu Yefu.

All because the Chinese are on a mission to wipe out the spiritual movement known as Falun Gong, or, as many refer to it, Falun Dafa—the teachings of the Great Law of the Universe. By the late 1990s, after it had been around for only a few years, Falun Gong comprised more members—estimates range from seventy to a hundred million—than the Chinese Communist Party.

Chunyan became a follower of Falun Gong in 1998, almost as a last resort.

For a couple of years, she had been having trouble sleeping, sometimes getting as little as two or three hours a night. Nothing was working. Anytime she felt the least bit drowsy, she went to bed, never certain when another chance for sleep might come around.

Wang Chunyune, her older sister and a Falun Gong practitioner, convinced her to give it a try.

Suddenly, dramatically, after she spent about two hours every day on five exercises along with meditation (reminiscent of ancient Buddhist and Taoist traditions), her health improved. And instead of thinking mainly of herself and the success she hoped to achieve, Chunyan began to think of others. A cousin told her before she took up the practice that her face looked scary, her muscles going the wrong way. Now, she seemed peaceful, happy.

Chunyan is sure she would have died if she hadn't become a follower.

Only being a follower wasn't enough. She felt an urgent need to spread the word about Falun Gong. If the practice could save her, it could save millions of others. Especially after the CCP went on the offensive in the summer of 1999 with all sorts of lies. Chunyan, who was well off by Chinese standards—she owned a company that sold chemical production equipment, with a yearly revenue of more than a million yuan (over $120,000 US)—bought a printing press to distribute flyers refuting those lies.

Which led to a life on the run.

"The buildings where I worked were under constant surveillance," she told me, through an interpreter. "I left to escape and was afraid to come home."

★ ★ ★

Li Hongzhi, a former government clerk, introduced Falun Gong to the Chinese people in the spring of 1992.

The practice was embraced across many strata of society, including by some of the CCP's highest-ranking political and military officials and perhaps, more importantly, their wives and children. In 1993, a foundation administered by the Ministry of Public Security awarded Li an honorary certificate. He traveled the country giving lectures and showing people how to perform the exercises. Today it seems almost impossible to believe, but in 1995 Li gave a lecture, his first outside China, at the Chinese embassy in Paris. The following week, the embassy sponsored a Falun Gong session.

However, as the movement grew in popularity, the government began to apply pressure on Li to set up a branch of the Communist Party within Falun Gong and charge fees.

He refused. Falun Gong has never had a political agenda and it has never been for sale.

That is the one of many things I admire about this group. No professional clergy. No formal membership. No places of worship.

Only peace-loving individuals united in a common purpose.

Last summer, I watched *Unsilenced,* a disturbing film about the Chinese government's crackdown on Falun Gong. I was struck with guilt once more. I should have done more to help these practitioners when I served in Congress and as ambassador-at-large for international religious freedom.

One line from the movie summed up the government position. It came from the official overseeing the tortures.

He was asked if Falun Gong was a big enough threat to warrant such treatment.

"If Falun Gong wins the people's hearts," he responded, "who will be left to follow the party?"

In 1999, party Secretary Jiang Zemin ruled that Falun Gong must be eradicated. Others in the party, including those who followed the practice, went along. What else were they going to do? This is China, remember, where dissent is not permitted.

Not if you want to keep your job. Or life.

A chain of events in the spring and summer of '99 explains how the crackdown came about.

In April, a critical article appeared in a university publication in the city of Tianjin, about two hours from Beijing. The writer, He Zuoxiu, a physicist, was the brother-in-law of Luo Gan, the country's head of public security. What a coincidence. Falun Gong practitioners were upset, and who could blame them? About five thousand showed up on campus a few days later to seek a retraction.

The demonstration was peaceful. Violence is against everything they believe in.

The police, however, didn't care if the protest was peaceful or not. They arrested forty-five followers.

Who were now faced with a difficult choice. Should they go home and let the process play out? Or should they take their case to the authorities in Beijing?

They went to Beijing.

Again, the demonstration, held on April 25, was peaceful, with more than ten thousand in attendance.

The practitioners were, *The New York Times* reported, "motionless, calm, and seated on the sidewalk."[38] The same day, a handful of them met with government officials who agreed to release the forty-five arrested in Tianjin. The crisis appeared to be over.

It wasn't.

Jiang wrote a letter to the members of the Politburo, claiming that the people behind the April 25 gathering were "planning and issuing commands." It was an outright lie. Right out of the CCP playbook.

Falun Gong doesn't have any leaders. It doesn't issue any commands.

Not long afterwards, Jiang referred to what took place on April 25 as "the most serious incident since the political turbulence in 1989." In other words, since Tiananmen Square.

On July 19, 1999, it became official. The Chinese banned the practice of Falun Gong. The next day, the arrests began.

The estimates of the number of those arrests range from a few hundred to more than five thousand. The CCP has been waging a brutal war against Falun Gong ever since.

How many have been imprisoned or sent to labor camps? Hard to say. Millions, for sure. Killed? Many thousands.

Which brings us back to Chunyan.

After she left her home in early 2002, Chunyan used prepaid cards at public phone booths to call her husband and set up times for the two to meet in secret at restaurants, coffee shops, and hotels.

They loved each other deeply, although, I was surprised to learn, it had been an arranged marriage. Chunyan was in her late twenties when her mother said it was time she got married and that Yu Yefu was the man she had in mind. He was caring and responsible, just like Chunyan's dad.

Yu Yefu never practiced Falun Gong, not even after his wife joined the movement. Nor did he help distribute flyers. Nonetheless, the police harassed him at his workplace, demanding to know where his wife was hiding out. He never said a word. Yefu occasionally brought their daughter, Yu Ping, who was in her late teens, to the meetings with his wife. The three tried to act like a normal family, for a few hours at least. When their lives were anything but normal.

The whole time, Ping thought her mom was traveling for business. Which was precisely what her mom wanted her to think.

"She was protecting me," Ping said.

However, when Chunyan was unable to reach her husband for three days, she went to the house, a risk she felt she had to take. When she arrived, she found Yefu unconscious on the couch with the gas turned on. She reached out to her sisters, who called for an ambulance.

The doctors performed one operation after another. To no avail.

Chunyan stayed away from the hospital, having been warned by her sister that there were "some people who look suspicious. Their movement is not normal inside a hospital."

Her husband was, literally, on his death bed, and she couldn't be by his side. It is difficult to imagine such inhumanity.

Soon after discovering the body, Chunyan called her daughter, who was in college about three hours away. However, instead of telling her the truth, she told her that her father had been injured in a car accident.

She was protecting her again.

Chunyan worried that if Ping knew her father had been attacked because of her mother's involvement with Falun Gong, she wouldn't be able to stop worrying: Would her mom be next?

Ping arrived at the hospital about three o'clock the following morning.

"I remember being in a dark hallway," she said, "thinking that if I could just run a little faster, my daddy will be okay. If I could just get to his bed and hold his hand."

Although he was almost fifty years old, she said the last time she saw him before the attack, he had looked thirty.

"It never occurred to me," she said, "that he would die. I thought he would live to a hundred years old."

At the funeral, Ping kept asking: "Where is my mom?"

Her relatives didn't answer. They tried to keep her busy.

Ping was mad, but she couldn't let herself get too mad. She had always been taught that moms were right, no matter what.

She was confused by the number of strangers who showed up for the service. *Are they my daddy's friends*?

They were not. They were police officers. Stationed everywhere, in case Chunyan made an appearance.

The doctor told Ping's two uncles that the amount of gas inhaled wasn't fatal. Something else caused his death. But what?

We will never know.

The officers told her uncles that if the family wanted to investigate the matter further, her mother would have to go to the police station and surrender.

The uncles never told Chunyan what the police said. They were afraid that if she were to go, the officers would harm her, as well. The police later ruled there was no evidence of foul play, that her father's death was a suicide.

During the cremation ceremony, however, an aunt showed Ping some black marks on her dad's skull, suggesting he was beaten. Always remember, her aunt told her, that your dad endured a terrible death.

The death of Yu Yefu caused a ripple effect in the family.

His sister had a heart attack and his father later committed suicide.

"I am joining my son," he said.

Chunyan went to prison, sentenced to two years. She was arrested three days after her husband was cremated. The police found her walking near a public square. A red sedan stopped, someone shouted her name, she turned around, and before she knew it, she was in the back seat. I've heard stories of a car in China pulling up to grab someone off the street more than a few times, and it is always chilling.

You won't believe what they asked Chunyan after she was captured. On second thought, knowing how vicious these people are, maybe you will.

Why didn't you attend the funeral?

She spent the first of her two years' imprisonment at a detention center in northeast China.

The guards taunted her constantly.

"Look at you now," they said. "You were wealthy and had a great career, but now you are in jail."

How Chunyan was able to survive is beyond me. God's plan, that's the only answer I've been able to come up with, in order that she could tell the world what is going on in China.

She told me the same thing Pastor Pan of the Mayflower Church said: She did not hate her oppressors.

The guards tried to get her to sign some documents renouncing her faith, something they attempted with every Falun Gong practitioner. Three other female prisoners, strong women in their twenties, were forced by the guards to beat her on the back with a three-foot-long club made of two iron rods twisted together.

After the beating went on for a while, Chunyan banged her head against a wall.

"Were you trying to kill yourself?" I asked.

No, she insisted. She was trying to show the women that no matter what they did, she would not renounce her faith.

Even so, the prisoners grabbed ahold of her. If they hadn't, she might have died that day. Her back was drenched in blood.

Another time, the authorities made her sit on a small stool for ten hours, maybe longer, in a circle they drew and told her she wasn't permitted to venture outside of it. Whenever any part of her body crossed the circle, they beat her. A thought occurred to me: *Why didn't she spare herself any further torture and give them what they wanted? Sign the stupid documents. Renounce your faith. It won't mean you are renouncing it in your heart.*

She couldn't do it. She couldn't lie.

Every month or so, her daughter came for a visit—ten, fifteen minutes tops—but it was better than not seeing her at all.

Ping noticed the change in her mother, and it was alarming. Gone was the confident woman she had always known, replaced by one full of fear, her eyes darting around the room.

Chunyan chose her words carefully while the guards were nearby, small talk for the most part. But when she rose from a chair, she whispered to her daughter, "I was beaten. Tell your aunt."

She said it three times.

When she emerged from the meeting room, Ping informed her aunt what her mother had told her.

Her aunt did not hold back.

"Do not hurt my youngest sister," she told the guards. "If you ever do that again, I will report your behavior to everyone, including the media I know and your superiors."

The beatings soon came to an end. Whether what Ping's aunt said to the guards was the reason is impossible to know.

Chunyan worked fifteen-hour days in prison, making clothes—she brought one of the jackets to our DC meeting in 2025—but at least she wasn't being tortured anymore.

In 2003, they gave her a blood test. She couldn't figure out why. Not until several years later, when she found out about the forced organ harvesting in China, did it dawn on her. They wanted to see if any of her organs might be a match for someone. Thank God they weren't.

When Chunyan mentioned the subject, I thought back to when I first heard about the organ harvesting.

It was in 2006. The news, which was hard to believe, came in a report from David Kilgour, a member of the Canadian parliament, and David Matas, a human rights lawyer, also from Canada.

The organs harvested have included livers, kidneys, spleens, and hearts, many taken from Falun Gong practitioners.

While they were still alive.

Ethan Gutmann, the senior research fellow at the Victims of Communism Memorial in DC, told me there have been between sixty and one hundred thousand organ transplants per year, primarily from individuals twenty-five to thirty-five years old, when they are in the prime of life and their organs have stopped growing.

How many people have been victimized? We can't be certain. He said up to six organs can be taken from a single prisoner.

Today, in 2026, it is still hard to believe.

How evil one must be to even think of such a gruesome scheme, let alone carry it out.

Still, the evidence is impossible to refute, the number of transplants extremely high for a supposedly voluntary system. And how can the Chinese know that someone is about to die and have the organ recipient ready...in the next room? Organs must be transferred within about twelve to sixteen hours to be viable.

Fast-forward to late 2018 and early 2019, when the China Tribunal, chaired by England's Sir Geoffrey Nice, who had been the lead prosecutor in the war crimes trial of Serbian President Slobodan Milosevic, interviewed more than fifty witnesses and experts.

Here was China's chance to offer evidence that the charges, which they had denied over and over, were false.

They couldn't do it.

The tribunal's ruling said it all: "Commission of crimes against humanity against Falun Gong and Uyghurs [has] been proved beyond reasonable doubt. Victim for victim and death for death, cutting out the hearts and other organs from living, blameless, harmless peaceable people constitutes one of the worst mass atrocities of this century."[39]

In 2021, Jin Renqing, China's former finance minister, died at the age of seventy-seven. Nine years earlier, he had received a heart transplant. As a friend of his put it, "Everyone joked that he was a 'sixty-eight-year-old man with a twenty-eight-year-old heart.'"

Very funny.

A year later, Gao Zhanxiang, the former deputy minister of culture, passed away. "He has replaced many of his internal organs," according to his obituary, "and joked that many of his 'parts' were not his own."

One final point about organ harvesting:

It appears that Western-based companies may be complicit. A 2019 report by the International Coalition to End Transplant Abuse in China concluded there were about two dozen Western companies that "support this business with their technology and products, and benefit from it financially, regardless of whether they are aware of it."[40]

I asked Chris Smith, who sponsored a bill against organ harvesting that passed the House in 2025 for the second time—the vote was 406–1—if it was possible the companies had no idea what their technology was being used for.

Absolutely not, he told me.

* * *

In 2004, Chunyan was released from prison. I wish I could tell you her nightmare was over.

It was only beginning.

Chunyan, who was shunned by many of her former friends—they avoided eye contact when they ran into her on the street—went back to printing the literature that disputed the lies the government was telling about Falun Gong.

This made no sense to me. She had already paid an incredibly high price. Why take the same risk again? She wasn't risking just her own life. She had a daughter to think about. Yet when I probed deeper, Chunyan didn't hesitate for a second. If she didn't tell the truth, who would? And if no one told the truth, the lies would become the truth.

Lo and behold, in August 2007, she was arrested again. The sentence was five years.

In November of that year, a guard gave her a message from Ping. She had a chance to go to America and be an au pair. What did her mother think?

What did her mother think?

Her mother was emphatic. "Please tell her to go immediately," she told the guard. It was the only way Ping could ever be free. The rest of her family felt the same way.

Yu Ping left and hasn't been back to China since.

For years, Ping wondered if she would ever see her mother again. Then, in May 2013, her mother called.

"I'm about to cross the border," she told her daughter.

"Cross what border?" Ping wanted to know.

"Don't ask."

The line went dead.

For the longest time—it was two days, but it seemed like forever—Ping was scared to death. Finally, her mother called again. She was on a bus from Myanmar to Thailand.

"I couldn't believe it," Ping said. "She never told me about any plan to leave China. There was no normal way for her to escape. She didn't have a passport."

As it turned out, Chunyan had reached out to members of an underground gang she had heard about from other Falun Gong practitioners. They would be the ones to smuggle her out of the country. The trip, which cost about $6,000 US, was like something out of a Ken Follett novel, Chunyan hopping on a motorcycle for the first time.

Was she worried about being robbed or raped by the gang members?

Not one bit. They had morals, which was more than she could say about the CCP.

Mother and daughter enjoyed quite a reunion in Thailand. They hadn't seen each other in five years.

In 2015, Chunyan, who had secured U.N. refugee status in Thailand, arrived in the United States.

Ever since, she has been spreading the word about Falun Gong. Would you expect anything different? A few years ago, she went from county to county collecting signatures in support of a resolution in the Virginia General Assembly critical of forced organ harvesting. The resolution passed 82–0.

Chunyan has never remarried. No one could replace the man she lost.

Part of me expected to be desensitized to her story. That after hearing heartbreaking accounts from Peter Xu and Arjia Rinpoche, and Mihrigul Tursun, the Uyghur woman whose story I'll share in the last chapter, nothing more could get through.

Quite the contrary.

Chunyan, as is typical of Falun Gong followers, wasn't interested in politics or regime change. All she wanted was to practice her faith in peace and for others to know the truth about Falun Gong. The faith that saved her life.

★ ★ ★

A few months after meeting Chunyan, I had a conversation with Cynthia Sun, a senior researcher at the Falun Dafa Information Center in Washington, DC. I wanted to find out where things stood with the persecution of Falun Gong.

Worse than I thought.

Because, ironically enough, the Chinese have failed miserably. Their goal was to get rid of Falun Gong in three months.

Today, almost three decades later, millions of people are followers of Falun Gong. The estimate is twenty million in China, but that is based on the activists alone; the total number of practitioners is no doubt much higher. And there are at least two hundred thousand print houses in the country that produce material similar to the flyers Chunyan distributed. Which is why the authorities have escalated their efforts to suppress Falun Gong. The number of followers harassed and detained—more than 5,600 in 2024—is the highest since the pandemic. So is the length of prison sentences, often between three and ten years. That's a death sentence for many practitioners, given their advanced age and the poor treatment they will receive.

The level of surveillance has also increased. Cynthia relayed the story of a practitioner who escaped from Shanghai in 2023. "She said she would go to an intersection," Cynthia explained, "and see fifty cameras on one utility pole, pointing in every direction."

I'm outraged by the escalation. Haven't these people been through enough?

I'm also heartened. Once more, their will and determination demonstrate the power of faith.

Even so, I can't help worrying about the future. With today's technology, the CCP has the ability to sway public opinion like never before.

The Chinese have an app, WeChat, that serves as a social media platform for more than a billion people.

They have put out a petition that appears to label Falun Gong and other banned religious groups as murderers, the usual lies. And told everyone, including elementary school students, they must sign the petition.

If they do, they will receive virtual badges that elevate their status in the community. If they do not, others will call them out, and who knows how that will impact their lives going forward.

As of 2024, tens of millions had signed the petition.

The authorities are reaching out to people who don't know anything other than what they have been fed constantly by the CCP, which erected the "Great Firewall of China," preventing internet access to uncensored sites. Google, Facebook, Twitter, and other Western internet companies have been banned.

You only have access to what the government wants you to see. If the public buys these lies, the time may come when there will be no one left to push back.

I told Cynthia about my conversations with Wang Chunyan. How she continued to print the flyers after her husband was killed and she was tortured in prison.

She wasn't surprised. If anything, Cynthia told me, Falun Gong followers such as Wang Chunyan become more motivated to spread the word. They want to show that their loved ones didn't die in vain. In the early years, practitioners were content to perform their exercises and meditation in homes or public parks, rarely taking part in any public activism. These days, however, now that they have been attacked by the government and shunned by society—in their schools, their companies, and so forth—this is the only way they can fight back.

For the first time, I began to grasp the difference between Falun Gong and other religions that are oppressed in China.

And why it poses such a big threat to the CCP's stranglehold on power.

First, the core principles of Falun Gong—truth, compassion, and tolerance—are basic tenets of the Eastern religions that most grandmothers in China taught and practiced in their families. They are the total opposite of the Communist ideology, which is focused on power and economic control.

Second, with so many practitioners being Han Chinese, the dominant ethnic group, Falun Gong appeals to a large percentage of the population, unlike the smaller Uyghur and Tibetan communities. And the fact it doesn't have leaders or a formal association makes it more difficult for the police and security officials to track down followers, even with the frightening advances in surveillance technology.

Falun Gong appeals to the yearning, especially among older people, for what was stolen during the Cultural Revolution. Otherwise, the movement would never have become so popular. It offers something the Chinese Communist Party cannot give its citizens in a million years.

Their old civilization. The one they cherished for generations. For centuries.

Civilization in China, with its many great accomplishments, was built on a blend of Eastern philosophies and religions such as Confucianism, Taoism, and Buddhism. Falun Gong simply seeks to reclaim those beliefs and practices.

As much as the CCP demands "Sinicization" of religion, Communism is the real carpetbagger, a failed ideology that was born in nineteenth-century Europe and has no natural connection to China.

There is no doubt in my mind that if there were a fair and free competition for the hearts and minds of the Chinese people, Falun Gong would prevail in a landslide. No wonder the Chinese government is so afraid.

One day, because of courageous individuals such as Wang Chunyan, the CCP will come crashing down.

Maybe not today. Maybe not tomorrow. But one day.

And when that day comes, the Chinese will have their great civilization once more.

Part Four

THE WAR ON THE UYGHURS

CHAPTER 10

THE COST OF FREEDOM

ENES KANTER FREEDOM, THIRTY-THREE YEARS old, fills me with hope for the future. Like Frances Hui, he chose a life of courage years ago, and there is no turning back. Speaking up for those suffering in China has cost him his profession—he was a basketball player—and a fortune. I can't think of many young men in his position who would have made the same choice.

His story, which he recounted in his 2025 best-seller, *In the Name of Freedom,* illustrates something that should terrify us. China's war on faith, as I can't repeat often enough, does not stop at China's border. It is also being carried out in the United States. By companies who are enforcing China's censorship in America.

First things first.

So much of what has made Enes the man he is today comes from his parents, Mehmet and Gulsum. That, too, he has in common with Frances.

One day, at age nine, Enes, living in Van, a city in eastern Turkey, was hanging out with a few friends who started to burn flags.

American flags.

"What are you doing?" Enes asked.

"We hate America," they told him. "Americans are evil. They are the Devil."

His friends gave Enes—he was Enes Kanter in those days—a lighter, a flag, and what amounted to an order:

Burn it.

Any other nine-year-old would have burned the flag without a second thought. That's what kids do to be part of the pack.

Not Enes.

"I looked at my hands and they were shaking," he told me. "I didn't know what to do or what to say."

As he fought through the fear, the words finally came.

"This isn't the right thing to do."

He threw the flag down and ran upstairs to find his mom.

"They're telling me to hate America and to hate Christians," Enes told her.

His mom wasted no time. "I'm not going to tell you what to do," she said, "but don't hate anyone before you meet them."

He promised he wouldn't. Enes has lived up to that promise ever since.

The other boys called him "the dog of America." From then on, his relationship with them would never be the same. Not long afterward, his parents left their small town and enrolled Enes in a school in Ankara, the capital. People were more educated in Ankara. They didn't grow up learning to hate America. They didn't join terrorist groups to fit in.

The school was part of the movement organized by Muhammad Fethullah Gulen, a noted cleric who believed education was the key to a more modern and tolerant Turkey. He called for the government to build more schools in addition to more mosques.

In school, the lesson Enes's mother had taught him was reinforced: Always search for common ground with others.

Yet as much as he valued education, he valued something else more.

Basketball.

His parents, not so much.

"My family did not want me to play basketball at all," said Enes, who took up the sport at age fourteen. He had tried soccer, Turkey's most popular sport, but was too tall and too slow.

It took a lot of convincing, but his father finally agreed. On one condition.

"You have to beat me one-on-one," Mehmet told him.

Easier said than done. Mehmet was six feet five. Enes was five feet seven.

For two months, Enes practiced outdoors on a concrete court with a hoop and no net. With a soccer ball. He didn't own a basketball.

"I watched clips of Michael Jordan and Shaquille O'Neal and Kobe Bryant," he recalled. "They were the only players I knew."

When the day finally arrived, Enes beat his father 5–3, with each basket worth a point.

His father was very impressed. His son put his mind to achieving a goal and worked as hard as he could, and it paid off.

"Like I promised," Mehmet Kanter said, "I will let you play. But I need you to become a good student before you become a good basketball player."

Deal.

Except Enes didn't become a good basketball player. He became a great basketball player.

He grew to six feet five in just two years, and after he played for the school team in Ankara, his father, now recognizing his son's potential, moved the family to Istanbul where, as Enes put it, "the big boys played."

At sixteen, he competed against guys twice his age. And beat them.

After he won an MVP award in France, Fenerbahçe, the top basketball team in Turkey, offered him a contract worth six million Turkish lira, the equivalent of $4.6 million US.

Enes was ecstatic. Until his father, one of the top scientists in Turkey, set him straight.

"You are not taking that money," he said. "You are going to America."

"What do you mean?" Enes responded.

"If you stay in Turkey, you are going to have to quit school, and your promise to me was education first."

Enes couldn't believe it. Nor could his coach, who asked him to write six million lira on a sheet of paper.

"I wrote it down," Enes told me, "but I didn't add the right zeroes. The coach said, 'You can't even *write* six million.'"

Enes appealed to his mother. Surely she would understand.

"I'm going to take that money," he told her. "I don't care what Dad said. The whole family will be set for the rest of our lives."

His mother was understanding. To a point. "I talked to him, too," she told Enes. "He wants you to finish your education."

That was the end of it. Enes wouldn't go against his father's wishes. A promise is a promise.

A few months later, Enes arrived in Henderson, Nevada, where he would play high school basketball.

He was excited about the journey ahead, although he couldn't stop thinking about the life he had left behind. *I turned down millions of dollars playing against thirty-five-year-olds, and now I'm going to play against kids?*

Or not.

Because of a deal with the shoe manufacturer, Nike, that he had agreed to in Turkey—his father signed the contract as Enes had yet to turn eighteen—he was considered a professional.

Other coaches said that if Enes were allowed to play, their teams wouldn't show up.

So much for Nevada.

The next stop was a prep school in Simi Valley on the outskirts of Los Angeles. Which presented more challenges.

"I walked into the classroom and there were spiders everywhere," he said.

But he was back on the court, where he belonged. The college coaches took notice, including the University of Kentucky's John Calipari. Kentucky has long been one of the top programs in America. Once again, however, Enes's past caught up with him. He told me that Nike and Fenerbahçe sent bank statements to the NCAA showing the money paid to his family.

The NCAA had no choice. Kentucky was out.

Enes was beside himself.

"It was tough, I'm not going to lie," he said. "I was about to become a superstar in Turkey, and now I couldn't play anywhere."

At least he had his faith. He's always had his faith.

God has a plan, he kept telling himself. If only He would tell him what the plan was.

Fast-forward to the summer of 2011 and the annual draft held by the National Basketball Association. Enes, who had been working out on his own—the NCAA had ruled he couldn't practice with his classmates—was the No. 3 overall pick by the Utah Jazz. Going to the Jazz turned out to the best thing that could have happened to him. In Salt Lake City, there weren't the distractions that existed in bigger cities. He could focus on basketball.

Lo and behold, fate intervened once more. A few weeks later, there was a lockout in the NBA—the players and management were fighting over the division of revenue and the salary cap—which would last until December.

No games. No practices. No contact with coaches.

What am I doing wrong? Enes wondered. *Maybe God doesn't want me to play basketball. Maybe I should quit.*

He didn't, needless to say, and looking back, he sees God's plan clearer than ever: He was preparing Enes for the struggles ahead.

There would be many.

In the fall of 2013, Enes sent out a tweet critical of Turkey's prime minister, Recep Tayyip Erdoğan, who had been involved in a massive corruption scandal.

Before long, the tweets came one after another, especially after Erdoğan shut down media outlets and put a lot of journalists and judges in jail. Just because Turkey was an important ally of the United States (a member of NATO, for goodness sake) doesn't justify for one second what Erdoğan did.

Some suggested Enes shouldn't have gotten involved in politics. I beg to differ.

This had nothing to do with politics. He was not telling people who to vote for.

This was about human rights.

His teammates—Enes had been with the Jazz for two full seasons by this point—warned him to be careful.

He couldn't be careful. Not when people's lives were at stake.

Still, he worried about the impact on his parents, who still lived in Turkey.

In 2015, he went back home for two weeks. To see family and friends and to clear up a few things.

"From now on," Enes told his parents, "I will be taking stances about what's going on in this country, and because of what I say you might get a lot of heat and hateful comments and might even be thrown in jail one day. If you guys are ready for it, great, then say so, but if not, let me know now."

It reminds me of Frances Hui and what her parents have had to endure. There is a steep price for demonstrating courage. No wonder we don't see more of it.

Enes's mother said exactly what I expected she would say.

"We are with you to the end," she told her son. "If you are speaking the truth and siding with innocent people, we support you no matter what."

Enes left Turkey with peace in his heart. To a point. He knew it might be the last time he would see his parents and his native land.

"People think I hate Turkey," he said. "That's not true. I just hate the Erdoğan regime."

The night before he left, he took his family to dinner at a restaurant by the water. He doesn't recall doing that before. They didn't talk about anything political. Only personal stuff. Everyone was happy to be together.

The cab to take him to the airport arrived early the next day.

Enes was right. In 2016, his parents received a lot of heat and hateful comments.

One time, when his mother reached the cashier at the supermarket, the guy spit in her face. "Your son is a terrorist," he said. "Get out of here."

His dad, meanwhile, was kicked out of the mosque and lost his teaching job at the university.

I think about the decision not to take the money from the Turkish basketball team. How different his father's life—and the lives of his whole family—would have been.

In August 2016, Mehmet Kanter disowned his son in a letter published by a pro-government newspaper.

"With a feeling of shame, I apologise to our president and the Turkish people for having such a son," the letter said. "His statements and behavior trouble our family. I told Enes that we would disown him should he not change his course. He did not care. I would not have taken Enes to the US for the basketball camp where his talent was discovered had I known that it would come to this point."[41]

Enes wasn't shocked. He knew the letter was written under duress. Even so, it stung to read the words in print.

Still, not believing the letter was genuine, the police showed up at his parents' house. They assembled everyone in the living room and tore the place apart, looking for any sign the Kanters were in communication with their son.

They found nothing but came back a short time later and hauled his father off to jail.

Enes was able to get the US government to apply enough pressure on Turkey to get him out.

Unfortunately, not quickly enough.

Something, it seemed, was done to him when he was in prison.

"He is acting very weird," Enes's brothers told him. "When we ask him about it, he never answers. He just watches the wall for hours and hours."

★ ★ ★

As the years rolled by, Enes continued to weigh in on the troubling events in Turkey.

Then came the fall of 2019 and the pro-democracy protests in Hong Kong.

Enes was playing for the Boston Celtics, his fifth NBA team, when Daryl Morey, the general manager of the Houston Rockets, sent out a tweet in support of the protestors: "Fight For Freedom, Stand With Hong Kong."

The reaction to Morey's tweet was strong—and not just from the Chinese.

"I don't want to get into a word or sentence feud with Daryl Morey," LeBron James told reporters, "but I believe he wasn't educated on the situation at hand."

Enes told me he was in a team huddle soon after Morey's tweet when a Celtics representative issued a warning to the players not to say anything about China.

Enes couldn't believe it. For years he had been speaking out against the attacks on democracy in Turkey, and no one had told him to shut up. If anything, they had encouraged him. That included his teammates, Commissioner Adam Silver, and the Celtics' owners.

"But when the conversation was about China," Enes said, "the whole thing changed."

Did it ever.

After responding to LeBron's tweet—Enes listed about ten ways in which Erdoğan and his thugs had cracked down on him and his family—he heard from his agent. The message was similar to the one from the Celtics official. Enes must not say a word. China was watching his Twitter.

A few months later, the pandemic put the world on hold.

That fall, shortly after the 2020 NBA Finals took place in Orlando, Florida, in what was known as "the bubble"—the Los Angeles Lakers defeated the Miami Heat in six games, with no fans allowed to attend—Enes held his annual basketball camp in New York.

One day, the kids, many wearing masks, lined up for pictures and autographs. A parent, however, had something else on his mind.

"How can you call yourself a human rights activist when your Muslim brothers and sisters are getting tortured and raped every day in concentration camps in China?"

To his credit, Enes didn't get defensive. "Sir," he said, "I promise I will get back to you."

He canceled everything he had scheduled for that day, went back to the hotel, and turned on his computer to read about the Uyghurs, one horrible story after another. He was overcome with guilt.

"All these years, I had this huge platform and I had talked about only one dictatorship," he said.

That was about to change.

He called his manager and asked him to find a survivor of a Uyghur concentration camp. Reading stories wasn't enough. Enes needed to hear from someone with firsthand experience.

The manager found a woman who fit the bill. Enes met with her a few weeks later.

In 2023, he told the story of that meeting to the Congressional-Executive Commission on China.

"I remember every word that came out of her mouth," Enes said, "the tears running down her cheeks."

In his testimony, he relayed how she had explained the methods of torture the Chinese applied—the gang rapes, forced sterilizations, abortions, all of it. Enes, who reads the Quran and prays five time a day, was taken aback when she told him she had been too scared to worship at home.

He asked the woman what he could do to help her.

"Nothing," she told him.

Enes couldn't believe it.

What, then, was the whole purpose of our conversation? he wondered.

"I don't need your help," she explained.

She went on, as Enes told the commission, to say: "I live in America. I can do whatever I want. I can say whatever I want. I can eat whatever I want. I'm free. Help those two to three million

Uyghurs who are in concentration camps, getting tortured and raped every day."

You got it.

One thing he definitely could do: write a message on his sneakers, similar to the messages of social justice that other NBA players wrote on their sneakers in the fall of 2020. They were incensed over the death of George Floyd, an African American, after an altercation with a white police officer in Minneapolis.

Enes's first chance came on October 20, 2021, in the nationally televised season opener against the New York Knicks at Madison Square Garden. He couldn't have asked for a bigger stage. Instead of referring to the Uyghurs, however, Enes put a different message on his shoes: FREE TIBET.

"I didn't want people to think, 'He only supports Muslims.'"

He put the shoes on during warm-ups and then joined the team huddle. The game was about to begin.

"Two gentlemen who worked for the Celtics came up to me," Enes recalled," saying, 'You got to take those shoes off.' I asked if I was breaking any rules. 'No,' they told me, 'but we are getting so many calls internationally and from the NBA.' I said, 'Even if I get fined, I'm not taking them off,' and they said, 'We're not talking about a fine; we're talking about getting banned.'" The Celtics' games would indeed, be pulled off Tencent, the Chinese streaming service.

Enes was sorry to hear about the ban, but he didn't regret wearing the sneakers. He was on the verge of becoming an American citizen—the big moment was set for November 29—and what could be more American than exercising his right to free speech?

He told me that someone from the National Basketball Players Association, the union that represents the players, called him after the game.

The message was loud and clear. He was to stop wearing the sneakers.

Again, he asked if he had broken any rules. Again, he was told no.

Enes told the commission on China that the players association, which called his manager every hour, said that if he didn't give in, it would change the rules so that no player would be allowed to put a message on his shoes.

Finally, Enes, who was bombarded with "media requests from countries I had never heard of," relented. He promised to never again wear a sneaker with the words FREE TIBET.

Two days later, at a game against the Toronto Raptors, the message on his shoes read FREE UYGHUR.

The union was furious, claiming Enes had lied. He could never be trusted again. (Technically, he didn't lie. The promise he made related to freeing Tibet, not freeing the Uyghurs.)

In any case, Enes didn't receive any playing time when he wore the FREE TIBET shoes, and he was on the floor for only the last five minutes when he wore the FREE UYGHUR shoes. After the first game, against the Knicks, Enes said his coach, Ime Udoka, told him that the lack of playing time had nothing to do with his sneakers.

Nonsense, according to Enes.

"I played every [preseason] game before that game," Enes said in one interview.

Even so, he wasn't deterred. In the fourth game of the season, against the Hornets in Charlotte, he wore shoes that read MADE WITH SLAVE LABOR. This was an obvious dig at the Hornets' owner, who had been closely aligned with Nike for nearly forty years.

His name was Michael Jordan.

With each passing day, Enes became more isolated. His teammates, who had been supportive when he criticized Turkey, treated him like a leper now that he was criticizing China. He said even his agent told him that if he were to say another word about the Chinese government, he would never play basketball again.

Enes hung up.

That was the end of their relationship.

Enes asked the players association for Adam Silver's phone number. It wouldn't give it to him. It was bowing out.

So Enes asked a teammate. The teammate agreed but, not wanting there to be any evidence that he was the one who gave out the number, opened his phone and walked away for a few minutes. Soon afterward, Enes and the commissioner had that talk. I wasn't on the call, so I can only take his word for it, but Enes claims that Silver told him he knew nothing about China banning the Celtics games on Tencent.

Fast-forward to February 2022 and the NBA trade deadline.

Enes had gotten back onto the court, eventually, though his minutes were way down from the year before.

On February 8, with twenty-four seconds left in a game against the Brooklyn Nets, Enes took a pass from Payton Pritchard and nailed a three-pointer from twenty-two feet.

"All my teammates were cheering," he told me. "I was sure this would be the last points of my career."

He was right.

Two days later, the Celtics traded him to the Houston Rockets, who soon released him.

Enes kept hoping his former teammates would send him a text to show their support.

Crickets.

"They were all scared," he said.

What if Enes were to mention a former teammate's name in an interview? The word would surely get back to China, and the player might very well lose his precious endorsement deals.

I cringed when I heard that.

Don't the players have enough money already?

As Enes once said to his teammates, "If your mother or sister or daughter was in those concentration camps and getting tortured every day, would you still take money over your morals?"

He got frustrated when his teammates put down America.

"I will buy you a first-class ticket to Iran, North Korea, or China," Enes told them. "'You criticize those countries, and you will be in jail,' I said to one of them. 'While you are playing basketball, people on the other side of the world can't find clean water to drink or food to eat.'"

Athletes he knew in other sports also demonstrated a lack of courage.

"They said they supported me," Enes recalled, "but wouldn't do it out loud. They, too, have endorsement deals and jersey sales."

In January 2023, not long after Enes met with Pope Francis at the Vatican, Turkey placed a $500,000 bounty on his head.

"That really bothered Turkey," he told me. "In their eyes, I am a terrorist. How can a terrorist meet with the pope?"

Still, he wasn't surprised, though like Frances Hui, the reality of having a bounty on his head hit him hard. He knew he would have to watch his back at all times, especially when he wasn't in America. "When I had a conversation with my friends on the ground," Enes told Tucker Carlson, "They said the mafia, the serial killers, actually, professional hitmen and cartels could be after my case. And I was speechless. I was like, 'This cannot be happening to an American citizen in U.S. soil.'"

Even before Turkey issued the bounty, Enes experienced some close calls.

In 2017, he was in Indonesia to give a basketball clinic for kids. At 2:30 a.m., there was a knock on the door of his hotel room. It was his manager. He hadn't come to talk about his contract.

"The police are looking for you," he said.

Having a strong suspicion that the Indonesian police would hand him over to the Turkish authorities, Enes bought a plane ticket within the hour and found himself in Romania, of all places.

Without a passport. It had been cancelled by the Turkish government.

Fortunately, thanks to the quick response of the US State Department, he was able to leave Romania for London a few hours later.

★ ★ ★

During the spring of 2025, I watched the NBA Playoffs.

LeBron James, at forty, still pulling off the impossible. Steph Curry, before he got injured, hitting shots from another county. The Knicks knocking off the Celtics, the defending champions, and so forth.

Only I couldn't help thinking about Enes and the life that was taken from him.

Enes, who could have made close to $50 million in his next contract, thinks about it, too.

"Those are still my brothers, my friends, the people I did battle with," he told me. "It breaks my heart."

Yet if he had to do it all over again, he wouldn't change a thing.

"What I'm doing," he said, "is bigger than basketball."

I'll say.

To me, there is only one solution:

The NBA must condemn the three genocides in China. In public and as often as humanly possible.

Believe me, I realize the NBA is a global business. But that is all the more reason it should use its platform for good, not evil, and what could be more evil than genocide? The Chinese money would dry up, but the league's stature would soar, proving Americans can't be bought off when it comes to standing up for religious freedom. The league would also give hope and encouragement to the Christians, Buddhists, Muslims, and Falun Gong practitioners. Like what happened in the 1970s and '80s when the Jewish refuseniks in the Soviet Union learned that others around the world were supporting their campaign to leave the country.

The CCP would pay a substantial price, as well, if it were to respond by banning NBA games on television. They love the NBA in China. I wouldn't be surprised if a ban led to protests in the streets.

Each of us, when we face our Maker someday, will have to answer the question: Did we do the right thing with the opportunities we had?

★ ★ ★

The NBA isn't the only industry that is failing this huge moral test.

So is Hollywood.

Do you know the last time Tinseltown released a major film that showed anything negative about China?

The answer: 1997.

The films were *Seven Years in Tibet* and *Kundun.* Since then, there has been nothing about the Uyghur camps, the Hong Kong takeover, or the persecution of the Buddhists, Christians, and Falun Gong.

Nothing.

And the last A-list celebrity to speak out against the CCP was actor Richard Gere, known for his roles in *An Officer and a Gentleman* and *Pretty Woman.*

Gere demonstrated great courage, and it wound up damaging his career.

At the Oscars ceremony in 1993, he presented the Academy Award for Best Art Direction. I've never been a fan of celebrities exploiting these occasions to bring up politics.

This was different. Too much was at stake. Still is.

Gere referred to "the horrendous human rights situation in China, not only toward their own people but to Tibet, as well," and expressed the hope that Deng Xiaoping would remove troops from Tibet and "allow these people to live as free, independent people again."

Bravo!

So why has Hollywood, so outspoken about other causes—the Palestinians, Native Americans, and so forth—been silent about this one?

Is it the money again?

A significant percentage of the film industry's box office receipts comes from the Chinese market. Also, let's not overlook the Chinese investors who have bankrolled their share of movies over the years. Hollywood has even, on occasion, allowed the CCP to edit out before release sections of films that it finds objectionable.

This can't go on any longer. The best storytellers in the world must use their talents to tell the truth.

About the forced organ harvesting. The treatment of the Uyghurs. The bishops in prison. Etc. etc. If nothing else, a movie about the amazing journey of the Mayflower Church, which would be the perfect feel-good vehicle for Hallmark.

Think of the impact Steven Spielberg could make with his skill and stature. He would have nothing to lose.

Hollywood must do something, and soon, to show it is not owned by a regime that, it bears repeating, has killed more of its own people than any other in history.

As for Enes Freedom, we haven't heard the last of him. Thank goodness.

He has announced his intention to run for Congress in 2030. He'll be eligible then, as the required nine years will have passed since he became a US citizen.

"This country has given me so much," he told me. To serve in government "would be a way of me thanking this country back." He claims to have one advantage over others who seek public office. Despite being forced out of the sport prematurely, he earned enough money "that I can't be bought."

Enes moves around freely in the US.

Freely but carefully.

He doesn't roam the streets, where he could be easily spotted. He travels, as he put it, from point A to point B, and wherever he goes, he alerts a small group of friends ahead of time. Just in case.

I'm reminded of something Enes told me in one of our last conversations. It has to do with his mother. The one who told him not to hate and to always look for common ground.

"Her biggest dream," he said, "was to watch me in the NBA."

He promised he would get her and his father the best seats in the house.

It never happened.

CHAPTER 11

A PROFILE IN COURAGE

NOTHING—THE MAGAZINE ARTICLES, THE TESTIMONY before Congress in 2018, the accounts of other Uyghur survivors, *nothing*—could possibly have prepared me for the story Mihrigul Tursun, in her mid-thirties, was about to tell.

A story I can't get out of my mind, and it has been well over a year.

A story, and I can't empathize it strongly enough, I do not *want* to get out of my mind. Nor, once you have heard it, and gotten a clearer sense of the enemy we are dealing with, will you.

I didn't expect to be so deeply affected when I met Mihrigul at a Washington, DC, office building one brisk evening in the fall of 2024.

Not at this stage of my life. I will turn seventy in a few months.

And not after the countless other stories I've heard during my decades in public service. (It is possible to believe, as I do with all my heart, in the goodness of God, who has been the foundation of my life since I found Jesus Christ at the age of thirteen, and in our goodness as His servants, and yet still recognize the evil man is capable of.)

I have seen women in Nepal who had been the victims of human trafficking in India, many sent back to their native land when they became too ill to be of any more use to their pimps. "She is dying," a nurse told me, pointing to a girl no older than sixteen with an advanced case of a sexually transmitted disease. "There is nothing we can do." The nurse pointed to another girl around the same age. "She is dying, too." I was devastated, thinking of my two daughters who weren't much younger at the time.

I have seen the ovens at Auschwitz. Everyone should visit a Nazi concentration camp. It is one thing to read about the Holocaust or see the archival footage. It is quite another to be there in person. You will never look at human nature and the world the same way again.

And I have seen the victims at a Rohingya refugee camp near Cox's Bazar in Bangladesh. One mother told me about her daughter who was tortured, a bayonet stuck up her vagina, while she and the girl's husband were forced to watch.

Anyway, after my conversation with Mihrigul, I phoned my daughter Abby from an Uber, and reached out as soon as I could to another daughter, Liz.

I called to share the horrors I had heard. To ask what they thought. What they felt. Both, being young mothers, were horrified to the core.

I thank God for how blessed my family is to live in a country where you can practice your religion and not be punished for it.

That's not the case with the Uyghurs.

★ ★ ★

At first glance, you would not be able to detect what Mihrigul Tursun has been through.

Mihrigul is beautiful, composed, engaging.

She told her story in English, to my surprise and delight. I have long relied on interpreters, but the pause while waiting for a translation often dilutes the impact of what has been said.

Her words were sometimes hard to make out, the tenses and phrases out of place. Which only gave her story more impact.

More horror.

In 2002, when she was twelve years old, she lived in a village in the province of Xinjiang in western China. One day the principal at her school announced that every student would have to take a special exam. Mihrigul studied hard for the exam. She didn't even do her chores. A few weeks later, she was called to the principal's office. Which was usually not a good thing.

The principal congratulated Mihrigul for recording the top score in the school.

Her blessing. And her curse.

A Chinese government official told her she would be rewarded for her performance by being invited to attend a boarding school in Guangzhou, roughly 2,500 miles away.

"This is a great honor," he told her.

Mihrigul didn't see it as a great honor. She would have to leave her parents and beloved grandmother behind.

Still, there was nothing she could do. Saying no to the Chinese Communist Party was not an option.

When the time came for the big move, she took a bus, meeting other children who would be attending the school, and then a train. The trip took five days. It was like being sent to another galaxy.

She was to be reeducated, stripped of her identity and dignity as a Uyghur so she could assimilate into the Han population, the country's largest ethnic group, and one day work for the government. The Communist Party was to be her God, they told her day after day. In the classroom, the lunchroom, everywhere. Not the God of the Muslim faith she and her family had long worshipped.

Mihrigul was scared to death from day one. What twelve-year-old wouldn't be?

During the first year, when she was one of about twenty-five Uyghurs in the school—the vast majority were Chinese—she cried. All the time.

And bared her soul on the rare phone calls she was allowed to make:

"Please let me come home, Daddy."

"No, you can't, my dear. The government has done a great thing for you and we should be grateful to them. This will lead to a wonderful life."

Her father had to say that. The authorities were listening, always. If they didn't like what they heard, he and the rest of the family would be under suspicion, and who knows where that would lead.

She wondered: *Do my parents love me? If they do, they wouldn't let me suffer like this.*

After a year went by, Mihrigul was allowed to go home.

For only twenty days. Taking into account the travel time, it was more like twelve.

During the second year, two girls, both twelve years old, killed themselves by jumping out of a third-story window, one just two weeks after the other. Mihrigul, who had been friendly with both girls, didn't say a word to her parents. The Chinese wouldn't let her. Like the Nazis, they have gone to great lengths to cover up their crimes.

As I listened to Mihrigul go back in time, reliving one horrifying moment after another, I no longer saw the face of a beautiful, composed, engaging woman. I saw a girl. In anguish.

I was overcome with guilt.

I'm so sorry to put you through this, I wanted to tell her. *You have suffered enough already. You're in the United States of America now. You are safe. You are free. Live your life and do what you can to put all this behind you. You don't owe anybody a thing.*

I didn't utter a single word.

Only through her testimony, I kept reminding myself, can we hope to put an end to what she and countless other Uyghurs have been forced to endure. And I had yet to hear the worst of it.

Did she think about jumping out of a window, as well? I asked.

Yes. What stopped her, she has no idea.

As the weeks, then months, dragged on, Mihrigul continued to write home, practically begging her parents to take her out of the school. The answer was always the same.

After the second year, she didn't go home. She worked at a supermarket near the school instead. There was no point in making such a long trip for such a short visit.

Mercifully, after five years, the Chinese let her go back to her village for good. They had done their job. She had been reeducated. She was ready to be a cog in the party machine.

Or so they assumed.

But faith—and I've seen this from one corner of the globe to another—possesses a power that is constantly underestimated. If anything, when someone tries to take a person's faith away, it becomes more powerful. It's like lifting weights. The more resistance, the bigger the muscles.

Some people may not want to take on a fight like that, and I pass no judgment on them. I have never been tortured. I can't pretend to know how I would react. That goes for all of us who are fortunate enough to enjoy freedom of religion.

Mihrigul never wavered.

"In my isolation," she wrote in *Place of No Return*, her 2023 memoir, "I turned more intensely to religion.... I think it was because this was one final link between me and my homeland."[42]

She would not remain in her homeland, however.

After working for an import-export company, she left China in 2010 for a university in Cairo, to pursue a Master's degree.

During the flight, she struck up a conversation with an Egyptian named Mahmud, who couldn't have been more friendly. He would later become her husband.

She cared for Mahmud a great deal, but there were also practical considerations for why they got married when they did. After being in Egypt for only a few months, Mihrigul received a summons to return to China. Being married to an Egyptian was the only way she could remain in Cairo. The wedding was in 2012.

In March 2015, she gave birth to triplets, two boys and a girl. Six weeks later, she and her husband and the children flew to China to meet Mihrigul's parents. She had promised to bring her kids there as soon it was feasible, and she was not one to break a promise.

However, when Mihrigul and her family arrived at the passport control center in Beijing, she was told Mahmud couldn't accompany them to their final destination, the city of Urumqi, because he didn't have the necessary visa. He told her to go on without him, that he would see everyone in a few weeks. Mihrigul was reluctant but ultimately agreed, though she couldn't imagine how she would be able to travel with three breastfeeding infants on her own. It was hard enough with her husband's help.

Thankfully, two strangers—a man and woman—came to the rescue.

"Your kids are so cute," they told her. "We are from Urumqi and speak some Uyghur. We'll help you."

It was an offer she couldn't refuse. The two sat next to her on the plane. They seemed like guardian angels.

Mihrigul took a nap.

When she woke up, she smiled at the woman.

The woman did not smile back. She and the man with her were police officers.

"You will get off the plane with us quietly, without saying a word to anyone," they told her.[43]

When the plane landed, Mihrigul and her children were escorted to a room in the airport. She sat at a table, two cameras capturing every moment.

"What is your name?" they asked.

"It is in the passport," she responded.

"Just answer my question."

She did.

Then came one question after another.

"What exactly will you be doing during this time in Xinjiang?

"Did you join a terrorist organization while you were in Egypt?

"Did you wear a headscarf?"[44]

After a few minutes, the police took the kids away. She screamed but it did no good.

Finally, after about three hours, there were no more questions. They taped her mouth shut and pushed her into a car so aggressively that they broke her nose. Within a half hour, she was in a room in an underground cell with metal bars. Strapped to a chair, she underwent another interrogation. It went on for twelve hours. It felt like twelve years.

How many Uyghurs were at her school? How many did she know in the whole country? How did she practice Islam?

Her answer was the same for every question: "I don't know."

Each time she said that, they yelled and beat her. She believes there were fifteen police officers in the room. Maybe more.

Mihrigul was in the police station for two and a half months, subjected to one interrogation after another.

The same questions. The same answers.

She prayed. Not for herself.

Please, God, give me just one chance to see my kids. I need to take care of them.

She was put in a cell with dozens of other women. The conditions were deplorable. To go to the bathroom, if you were lucky enough to get permission, you had to relieve yourself in front of everyone else. As for sleeping, since there was very little room, about two-thirds of the women had to try dozing off while sitting up. A few hours later, the women switched positions, giving a different third of the group the chance to lie down.

If that wasn't humiliating enough, everyone was woken up at 6:00 a.m., forced to march in place and sing the national anthem for a half hour, maybe longer, and after visits to the toilet and breakfast (a cup of rice and water), it was time for more indoctrination. They were forced to memorize every word of *Quotations from Chairman Mao Tse-tung,* filled with Communist Party propaganda and slogans. Prisoners were forced to recite different sections. If they got one word wrong, they were beaten.

One day, without warning, the nightmare ended. For the time being. It has never really ended.

Mihrigul was told she would be released, though she would be placed under house arrest. One false move and she would be back in jail, as would members of her family.

The authorities kept her passport, ID card, and cell phone. It was as if she didn't exist.

Before they let her go, she was forced to sign a document verifying she had received all of her personal items. It was a lie, of course, but she would have signed anything at this point. Anything to see her children again. Who, she soon found out, were in the hospital.

One hell was ending.

Another was about to begin.

At the hospital, a nurse handed Mihrigul her son, Moez. Then her daughter, Elena. Meanwhile, Mohaned, the third baby, had to remain in the Intensive Care Unit with respiratory problems.

She was in no mood to be patient.

She wanted to see her son.

Visiting hours were over, they said. She would have to come back tomorrow.

Mihrigul argued, but to no avail.

She got little if any sleep that night and it wasn't only because she hadn't seen Mohaned. She had also noticed cuts on the necks of her other two children. When her father called the hospital that evening, he was told the cuts were made because the children hadn't wanted to drink their formula and needed to be fed artificially.

Another lie.

The next day, Mihrigul and her father were greeted by a nurse and two doctors. Her son was dead, they said. He wasn't strong enough.

As the horror Mihrigul had been through began to sink in, my mind drifted and I lost track of some of the details. Her son was dead, that was all I could think about. Not because he wasn't strong enough. Because the Chinese had killed him.

A part of Mihrigul couldn't accept the truth. When she later touched her son's cold body, she asked her father for a blanket. "Wake up," she told Mohaned, "I need to feed you."

She was filled with rage.

"I wanted to kill them all," she told me, "to destroy all of the Chinese government."

While waiting in the hospital, her father cautioned not to say a word, or they might put her back in prison.

She somehow held it together. A miracle, if you ask me.

Soon it was time for another long journey, this one by bus, covering about 750 miles to the Taklamakan Desert.

Under Islamic tradition one must bury the body as quickly as possible, but it was difficult to find an imam willing to recite the necessary prayers. They were afraid something would happen to them if they were to officiate at the funeral of a boy whose mother was considered the CCP's enemy. Who could blame them?

Fortunately, her father found two who agreed. Not out of the goodness of their hearts. For a fee of $200, a huge amount of money for her family.

Mihrigul remained in the car during the brief ceremony. She couldn't bear to see Mohaned put in the ground.

"I couldn't accept that my son had died for a long time," she wrote in her memoir. "I still cannot, even to this day. Whenever someone asks me how many children I have, I always tell them three. And whenever their birthday comes around, I always buy three presents. I collect the gifts for my firstborn in a box and store them away."[45]

Before long, Mihrigul was placed under house arrest.

The police kept asking questions. Always more questions.

They gave her a cell phone that she was required to have on all the time so they could track where she was and listen in on her conversations. To make sure she wasn't practicing her faith.

In April 2017 (keep in mind that during this whole time, by this point almost two years, Mihrigul couldn't get word to her husband of what was going on), four officers came to the house and took her away.

Another underground cell. Another interrogation.

She was strapped to a bench, a board put under her feet to increase the tension, the pain.

What barbarians.

It went on for hours, and whenever she closed her eyes, even for a split second, they beat her.

In the earlier interrogations, she didn't admit that she prayed to Allah. This time, she did.

What was the point of holding back any longer? She was going to die anyway.

The officers got angry, attaching electrodes to her hands and feet.

"Excruciating pain shot through me from top to bottom, momentarily robbing me of my ability to breathe," she wrote. "The men watched as my body twitched, then they sent another shock through me that was a little stronger than the first."[46]

She pleaded to Allah, "Kill me!" This made the officers more angry. They sent more shocks.[47]

They soon put her in another camp where the conditions were even worse than the first one.

Women collapsed in the cell just about every day. In two months, she believes about a dozen died.

When they let her go, she was told that she couldn't say a word to anyone about what went on in the camp. She knew the drill. Except there was a different twist this time. She was escorted home by two Chinese officers who would now be her "relatives." They would live with her and her family.

The first evening was one she will never forget. Her father started to set up a space for the two men in the living room.

As he would for any relatives.

Only they didn't want to sleep in the living room. They wanted to sleep in the bedroom. Mihrigul, her aunt, and the two children slept with one officer, her father with the other. Her only refuge was the bathroom, and she didn't feel safe there, either, worried there might be cameras or a microphone to catch her if she tried to recite her prayers.

Her prayers would have to be recited in silence, as they have been by so many Uyghurs since the crackdown began.

Even so, her faith was stronger than ever.

The "relatives" didn't leave her alone. One followed her into the kitchen, putting his arms around her while she opened the fridge. She threatened to complain about him to his superiors. He laughed, saying his superiors wouldn't care one bit. If anything, complaining might send her back to prison. The next day, he ran his hands under her dress and fondled her breasts. Another morning, she woke up with the man's hand in her hair.

She thought of killing him. Or killing herself. Or both.

A knife, it occurred to her, would do the trick, except there were only two knives in the house and they were attached to a chain in the kitchen. The Chinese authorities—they thought of everything—had taken away the other knives, as they did in all the homes owned by the Uyghurs.

That didn't stop a woman living in the apartment upstairs. One night, the Chinese "relative" in that apartment raped the woman's eight-year-old daughter. Mihrigul heard everything. And then nothing. And then a scream. The mother had killed the man. The police took her away, and Mihrigul never saw her again. The daughter, either.

There was one more interrogation to come.

In November 2017, four officers showed up in the middle of the night to take Mihrigul away. Before long, she was in another cell, which she would occupy for weeks.

One day, she was taken to a room where she learned her fate.

"There are two options for your death," the officer told her. "You may choose to either be shot or to receive a lethal injection."[48]

The shooting would be quicker, he told her, but each bullet—and there would be three—would cost her. She didn't have the money. Lethal injection it would have to be. When this was going to take place, she had no idea.

One night, she had a dream. She was in the village where she grew up. There were no interrogations. No beatings. No "relatives."

Only peace and quiet.

The sky opened and she was flying. *Maybe they won't kill me,* she thought. *Maybe I will see my children again.*

★ ★ ★

Mihrigul Tursun has been a free woman for more than seven years—*free* being a relative term.

In the end, she was spared because her husband tracked her down in time to get her out of China. After he was denied a visa by the Chinese embassy in Dubai, where he worked, Mahmud filed a complaint with the Egyptian Foreign Ministry. It took forever, but the Egyptian authorities came through.

She thought he would never come back. That he had forgotten her.

"How could I forget you?" he told her.

Mahmud explained to government officials that his children were Egyptians. Thank God Mihrigul had left their birth certificates behind in Cairo when she went to China in 2015.

One day, the call came that he had been waiting for.

"I dropped everything," he told her, "and flew straight out here to you."[49]

Except, and I know I keep saying this, her ordeal was far from over.

They went to Cairo, but after a short time he had to return to his job in Dubai.

His company sued him for being gone so long without permission. Worse yet, the police took away his passport.

Not long afterward, Mihrigul received a call from her father, who said she should return to China. China was her home. Not Egypt.

She knew he had been forced to say that and that a Chinese officer was there with him.

"Nobody did anything to you," her father told her. "So stop your shenanigans...or do you want to ruin your entire family? Do you know how many of us are in trouble because of you?"[50]

Mihrigul was overwhelmed with guilt.

"It left me feeling very confused and doubtful as to whether I had done the right thing," she wrote. "The long arm of manipulation had even reached me thousands of miles away from the Chinese prison cells."[51]

One day, she heard from a woman at the US Embassy in Cairo who suggested they meet that afternoon at a McDonald's a few blocks away.

I'll be there, Mihrigul said.

At first she had thought about not answering the phone, the number being one she didn't recognize. She had received calls from the Egyptian police, who had spoken to the Chinese and wanted her to show up for questioning.

She had answered enough questions for a lifetime.

The woman didn't show up alone. She brought an interpreter and a colleague from the embassy. Mihrigul didn't trust them. How could she trust anyone at this point? So instead of hanging out at the restaurant, they went for a walk. That was Mihrigul's idea. Anything to make her more comfortable.

The Congress in the United States needed to know more about what China was doing to the Uyghurs, the woman told her. Would she come to America and tell the members her story?

In return, the US would grant her asylum. A new life.

"I was speechless," Mihrigul wrote. "Had Allah once more heard my desperate prayers?"[52]

In November 2018, Mihrigul appeared before a congressional committee chaired by then-Senator Marco Rubio.

The room was packed. She told them everything, including what the Chinese had done to her son.

"I could suddenly feel his swaddled body in my arms," she wrote. "Tears welled in my eyes, and I gazed into the faces of the members of Congress and saw their horror as well."

They had some questions, which terrified her. Not the questions themselves. What they reminded her of.

"I subconsciously expected to be punished," she wrote, "for them to inflict pain on me. What would happen if I didn't know the answer to one of their questions? I kept wondering."[53]

She gathered herself together and delivered the answers without fear. It gave her a lot of satisfaction to tell her story in such an important forum. But let's not fool ourselves. Mihrigul will never be whole again. "There will be no more happiness in my life," she wrote. "The Chinese government tortured me too much for that. They robbed me of the joys of motherhood, of the experience of holding my babies to my breast and being there for them.... Even the powerful American politicians couldn't give this back to me any more than they could bring back my deceased son or the family I'd been forced to leave behind."[54]

★ ★ ★

I spoke to Mihrigul a second time on January 20, 2025, hours after Donald Trump was inaugurated as the forty-seventh president of the United States.

"What would be your message to the new government?" I asked her.

"Please help my fellow Uyghurs," she said at first, but then got increasingly angry.

Her message would be the following:

- Never trust the Chinese government.
- Stop doing business with China.
- Every Chinese person who comes over here is a spy.

I was struck again by her courage in speaking truth and speaking it boldly.

Mihrigul, who works as an admission coordinator for a health care system, hasn't heard from her family in China, with the exception of a brief call with her sister, for over four years. In 2021, her parents sent a video and again told her to come home—and, again, she knew they had no choice but to say that.

"I just hope my father and mother forgive me," she said.

I told her about the guilt I had felt in asking her to relive her past. She wouldn't hear of it.

"I think of all the young girls who go through my fate," she said, "and all the others to come if I remain silent."

For the longest time, she was afraid. Even in America. A Chinese woman moved into her neighborhood in Arlington a few years ago. A coincidence? Mihrigul wasn't so sure.

She's friendly with other Uyghurs in the DC area.

To a point.

They know what the Chinese government thinks of Mihrigul. And while they may say hello in private, they keep their distance in public, not inviting her to weddings or other gatherings, worried about themselves and the families they left behind if word were to get out. She doesn't fault them one bit. She feels sorry for them, and so do I.

I asked about her two children. In her book, Mihrigul wrote that they were afraid of strangers, hiding from them on occasion. That's not the case anymore, I was relieved to find out. They have adjusted to life in America. They have a future.

As long as their health holds up.

Both have undergone one surgery after another, too many to mention, all stemming from what they went through at the hospital in China. Mihrigul continues to have difficulties, as well. She has almost no hearing in her right ear and the doctors have told her it will never get better.

Her kids, she mentioned in January 2025, still didn't know the truth about Mohaned.

"He likes to stay with your grandmother in Egypt," she told them.

"When will you tell them?" I asked.

"When they are stronger and more powerful," she said.

Putting her family's life back together wasn't easy, to say the least. Soon after Mahmud arrived in America, Mihrigul told him he should go back to Egypt and find a woman who wouldn't be damaged forever and could give him more children. She couldn't because of the procedures she was forced to undergo in the camps.

"I don't need any more babies," he told her. "Two babies are plenty."

Damaged or not, she was the woman he loved, and he would protect her from here on. When Mihrigul feels depressed, which is quite often, he drives her to see the White House and Capitol.

To remind her she is in America and not China.

She tells Mahmud the trips help, but she is lying. Even he doesn't know the full extent of her pain, her lack of joy. She can't bear to tell him.

Mihrigul would never commit suicide—it's a sin, and besides, she would never do that to her kids—but "sometimes I pray for God to take me."

In April 2025, she had me over for lunch at her apartment.

She prepared enough food—noodles, meat, desert—for the whole Congress. I wasn't hungry, but I couldn't say no.

She told me about a dream she'd had the night before, when she woke up screaming.

"Some people were coming to take me from home," she said.

It wasn't the first time she'd had that dream and, I dare say it will not be the last.

I asked again about her children.

They know the truth now about the brother who was killed. Her husband had told them on March 15, the day they turned ten. They couldn't go on not knowing forever. Her daughter took it as well as could be expected. Her son did not.

"I always thought I would have another brother," he said, "but now I am alone. Why did you lie to me, Momma?"

No wonder I can't get her story out of my mind and why I don't want to.

I often think of her infant son who was killed and ask God, *How could You let that happen? And while we're at it, how could You let the Chinese inflict so much pain on millions of other innocent Uyghurs? You are a loving God. You could stop this evil at any moment. Why don't You?*

I don't have the answers, and I may never have them this side of Heaven. All I know is that because of Mihrigul Tursun and others like her, the truth is coming out. Which gives me reason to hope.

For the day when the Uyghurs will be free to live without fear on the land they love and pray to the God they believe in.

AFTERWORD

THE INDIVIDUALS I PROFILED IN this book are often in my thoughts and prayers.

One day my mind drifts toward Mihrigul Tursun and her newborn child who was killed by the Chinese.

Does she still wake up in the middle of the night screaming? Does she still tell herself it might be best if God were to take her away?

I hope not. Mihrigul has so much to give. To her husband and her two other children. And to the world that needs to hear her story.

Another day, I think of Pastor Pan, who, overcoming his own insecurities, led the members of the Mayflower Church on a daring escape to an island in South Korea, then to Thailand, then Texas.

Is his congregation as unified as ever? How are he and his fellow parishioners adjusting to life in America?

Or, I pray for Frances Hui, the twenty-six-year-old activist who fled from the land she loved and has a bounty on her head.

Will she ever see her parents again? Will Hong Kong ever be free again?

I think about Peter Xu, Arjia Rinpoche, Wang Chunyan, Enes Freedom—all of them, really, from time to time. About what they have been through and what may lie ahead.

They were under no obligation to bare their souls. They have put themselves and their loved ones at risk once again, and for that I am truly grateful. I hope their stories accomplish the change they seek for the land they left behind.

We should all be grateful that they didn't remain silent.

Their voices, along with countless others—Cardinal Joseph Zen, Bob Fu, Congressman Chris Smith, the list goes on and on—give us hope that this evil empire, like the Soviet Union before it, will one day be no more and that people of faith in China will be free to worship without fear. Those in the fight for religious freedom get discouraged every so often—I certainly have—but not for long. Each display of courage is a reminder that even in a world too often controlled by the darkest forces, it is the individual, through the grace of God, that can bring down the mightiest oppressors.

The Chinese Communist Party has disqualified itself from global leadership by its hatred of faith. Its system will fail because it fails the human spirit. Indeed, the seeds of its own demise have already sprouted and are growing. We should water and fertilize them.

As ambassador-at-large for international religious freedom for three years, and as a United States senator for fourteen, I advocated for the victims of religious persecution in China and elsewhere, but there was never a moment to take it all in. To think of the human beings at risk. Their hopes, their dreams, their fears.

But now, having met these unsung heroes, I can attach names and faces to the suffering, and I believe this will help me be a more forceful advocate in the mission God has called me to at this pivotal moment in our time.

I think, as well, of how our society defines courage, and how often we get it wrong.

Courage is not overcoming an injury on the playing field. Or making a risky financial investment.

Courage is putting one's life on the line for something bigger than oneself. Something eternal.

I am a person of faith, reading my Bible, saying my prayers, confessing my sins, meeting in fellowship with other believers. Not until recently, though, have I truly pondered the consequences I might face for following my heart in a life-or-death situation, as has been the case with so many people of faith in China.

Thinking about that has led me to a clearer understanding of faith.

Not of how to preach it. Or live it. But of how to be willing to die for it.

As I got to know each of these heroes, I asked myself, *Would I have acted as courageously if I had been in their position?* I would like to think the answer is yes, but I really have no idea. None of us do. I know this: Their stories, detail by detail, have enabled my faith to grow more than I ever imagined. I pray that those stories have the same effect on you.

Most of us take our freedoms for granted. The freedom of religion, above all.

Which I find incredible, considering where this country would be today if religious freedom hadn't been guaranteed by the Founding Fathers in the First Amendment to the Constitution: "Congress shall make no law respecting an establishment of religion, or prohibiting the free exercise thereof."

The first Americans came from a Europe that was ridden with religious divisions, and there were the same divisions in the colonies: Anglicans in Virginia, Quakers in Pennsylvania, Puritans in Massachusetts, and Catholics in Maryland. Which is why the bold experiment of a free, democratic nation in the New World could have fallen apart at any time and why, in an act of Divinely inspired genius, our Founding Fathers chose not to establish a national Church and to guarantee the right to practice any faith, or none at all.

It is the most important freedom we possess. The freedom of the soul.

The yearning for that freedom exists in every human being, which explains why the Chinese authorities, despite all their might, have failed to win their war on faith.

Yet the war is far from over.

What I said before bears repeating: The CCP is intent on destroying Western civilization and replacing it with the China World Order of communism, atheism, and totalitarianism. Its business model is to help dictators become better dictators.

★ ★ ★

So, what can we do to win this war?

For starters, we have to admit we are *in* a war. That's something that too many people don't seem to grasp.

I'm reminded of what Ronald Reagan wrote in 1961 in reference to the Cold War with the Soviet Union: "The inescapable truth is that we are at war, and we are losing that war simply because we don't or won't realize that we are in it."[55]

We live in a world that chooses to ignore evil. Even when it is staring us in the face.

Because once we stop ignoring it, we have to do something about it, and that is a burden many of us, dealing with enough troubles of our own, do not wish to take on.

We must hold the Chinese responsible for every human rights abuse we uncover, at home and abroad, and make them pay a heavy price for their wrongful acts. We must also bring those abuses up with our friends and our enemies. Until something is done about them. It saddens me to no end how many leaders around the world don't make the Chinese Communists' crimes against humanity a priority. That includes countries in the Middle East who say nothing about the genocide against the Uyghurs.

Their fellow Muslims.

Again, follow the money.

"Some of them told us openly that we know what is happening," said Omer Kanat, executive director of the Uyghur Human Rights Project, "but we can't do anything because we have good relations with China."

I became so frustrated with one Muslim leader that I finally blurted out, "I'm a Christian and I think I care more about the Uyghurs than you do."

His answer was most revealing: "The Chinese play rougher than you guys do."

If that's the problem, we need to play rough, too. Because if we keep placing economic concerns before moral concerns, the war on faith will be lost, and China will win the world.

China needs a close economic relationship with the US. That is something we can exploit.

I agree with Chris Smith, who argues that we need to link progress on human rights in China to potential trade deals. Speaking of Smith, his House bill against forced organ harvesting needs to become law. People in China are being killed for their organs. We must do everything we can to stop this barbaric practice.

I meet a lot of individuals who have accomplished amazing things. Yet it never ceases to disturb me how little, if anything, they know about the atrocities being committed in China.

How can that be? I wonder. In an age where there is no shortage of media.

Because the media, with the exception of a few conservative and Christian outlets, has largely ignored what's happening in Tibet and with the Uyghurs, Falun Gong, and Christians. Chris Smith told me he has held 107 human rights hearings on China, to which the media has responded, as he put it, with "crickets."

The media claims there has been a genocide going on in Gaza but ignores the three genocides in China. That's a huge failure on their part.

The Vatican must also speak out.

As I explained earlier, Pope Leo needs to call out China, and demand the release of the incarcerated bishops. Rome, not the CCP, must be allowed to pick the bishops in China. The pontiff should travel to the Republic of China (Taiwan), a country it has diplomatic relations with, and, in the spirit of Pope John Paul II, tell the Chinese people, "Be not afraid."

President Trump, meanwhile, should convene a White House summit with members of all faiths to come up with a plan to make religious freedom a reality throughout the world, including in China.

Not only for moral reasons. For strategic reasons, as well.

The White House, by statute, is required to put together a National Security Strategy (NSS), that alerts Congress to the most substantial threats we face.

In the next NSS, we should focus on the religions persecuted by the CCP and make the free exercise of faith an essential security objective in our battle with China. The Chinese people are our natural allies in combatting the CCP's war on faith.

A war that, it must be noted once more, the Chinese aren't waging only on their own soil. They are waging it around the world, including in the United States. It's known as transnational repression, or, as former Congressman Mike Gallagher aptly called it, "transnational terrorism." The goal is to intimidate and to silence voices of dissent.

Here is an example that involves Mihrigul Tursun.

Mihrigul was in New York two years ago, about to address a workshop on genocide, when the phone rang. It was her sister, calling from Xinjiang. The two hadn't spoken in nine years. Mihrigul was so suspicious about the call that she hung up. It turned out a Chinese man had, indeed, been on the line and the phone soon rang again.

"We know what you're doing," the man told Mihrigul.

He even knew the table where she was sitting.

Mihrigul wasn't intimidated one bit.

"Are you here? Then shoot me," she said. "I'm not scared of you."

Another example is the US-based Shen Yun performing arts group, who have received bomb threats and death threats.

This harassment must end and anyone who participates in it should be prosecuted to the full extent of the law.

Also disturbing, as I stated before, is how many former members of Congress and former congressional staffers are working for the CCP. The solution is to ban the lobbying of Congress by China as long as the CCP is in power.

Back to the president.

The issue of religious freedom around the world would be catapulted forward by a prime-time presidential address to the nation. President Trump has made it clear that "we need more religion."

Well, the best way to get more religion is to have more religious freedom.

The speech could be along the lines of the one President Kennedy delivered about civil rights in June 1963. Kennedy declared civil rights to be a "moral issue," not just a constitutional one, and said that the country could not truly be free until everyone was free.

Also extraordinarily helpful would be President Trump and others in his administration bringing up religious freedom at major international forums.

At the United Nations, the G20, the G7. All of them.

The world must know where we stand. China must know where we stand.

The president, vice president, members of the Cabinet, and members of Congress should meet with the victims of persecution.

Imagine a meeting with Li Hongzhi, the founder of Falun Gong.

Xi Jinping and the Politburo would go berserk. Let them. We have to act boldly and not worry about how they will react. Think of the boost it would give to the millions of Falun Gong practitioners. There would be a surge of activity, and more important, a surge of hope. Religion, I must repeat, poses the greatest threat to the CCP, and that is because it is so much a part of the Chinese civilization. And the religion the CCP fears the most is Falun Gong.

In 1983, when Natan Sharansky, the Jewish refusenik who was confined in an eight-by-ten-foot prison in Siberia, read that Ronald Reagan had referred to the Soviet Union as an "Evil Empire," it changed everything.

"By tapping on walls and talking through toilets," Sharansky wrote, "word of Reagan's 'provocation' quickly spread throughout the prison. We dissidents were ecstatic ... the leader of the free world had spoken the truth—a truth that burned inside the heart of each and every one of us."[56]

Finally, what the Chinese refer to as Xinjiang is East Turkistan, a mostly Muslim country that is not, or should ever be considered, part of China. The same applies to Tibet, a primarily

Buddhist nation, that has been swallowed up by China the way Armenia, Lithuania, and Kazakhstan were swallowed up by Russia into the Soviet Union.

That's what Communism does. It gobbles up its neighbors on the way to taking over the world.

The Dalai Lama has offered for Tibet to be part of China if it is granted autonomy to run its own affairs. While I doubt his Middle-Way Approach will work, if Tibetans want to try it, that is their choice. As I indicated in chapter 7, if the CCP won't go along, we should call for Tibet's independence.

As for Hong Kong, the rights it long possessed under the guidelines of "one country, two systems" must be restored. Immediately.

Or we should call for its independence, as well.

★ ★ ★

Everything on earth, the Tibetan Buddhists believe, is temporary.

I couldn't agree more.

Which is why I burned my resume all those years ago.

And why I'm filled with hope about the future of religious freedom in China.

God will play the lead role, but He won't do it alone. We must each do our part, like the heroes I profiled have done theirs.

As a priest once told me, "Do what is put in front of you to do and leave the results to God."

ENDNOTES

1 Arjia Rinpoche, *Surviving the Dragon: A Tibetan Lama's Account of 40 Years of Chinese Rule* (Rodale, 2010), 34.
2 Revelation 1:9 (New International Version).
3 "As for you, you meant evil against me, but God meant it for good, to bring to pass, as it is this day, to save many people alive." Genesis 50:20 (World English Bible).
4 Psalm 100:1–2 (Amplified Bible).
5 *The Wall Street Journal,* June 2, 2021
6 Pan Yongguang, "An Exodus From China," interview by Sam Hine, *Plough* 42 (October 2024), https://www.plough.com/en/topics/justice/human-rights/an-exodus-from-china.
7 Psalm 126:1–2 (New International Version).
8 Pan, "An Exodus."
9 2 Chronicles 16:9 (New American Standard Bible).
10 Pan, "An Exodus."
11 Ellen Bork, "The Struggle for Freedom: The Christian Pastor Convicted of Subversion against the Chinese Regime," George W. Bush Presidential Center, April 2, 2024, https://www.bushcenter.org/publications/the-struggle-for-freedom-the-christian-pastor-convicted-of-subversion-against-the-chinese-regime.
12 AsiaNews.it. "Liao Yiwu: Save the Life of Pastor Wang Yi. He Risks Dying like Liu Xiaobo." CHINA, www.asianews.it/news-en/liao-yiwu:-save-the-life-of-pastor-wang-yi.-he-risks-dying-like-liu-xiaobo-46476.html. Accessed 16 Jan. 2026.
13 Carter, Joe. "5 Facts about Persecuted Chinese Pastor Wang Yi-Erlc." 5 Facts about Persecuted Chinese Pastor Wang Yi, erlc.com/resource/5-facts-about-persecuted-chinese-pastor-wang-yi/. Accessed 16 Jan. 2026.
14 Yi, Wang. Edited by Hannah Nation and J.D. Tseng. *Faithful Disobedience: Writings on Church and State from a Chinese House Church Movement.* page 154. IVP Academic. December 6, 2022.

15 Ibid.
16 Yi, Wang. Edited by Hannah Nation and J.D. Tseng. *Faithful Disobedience: Writings on Church and State from a Chinese House Church Movement.* page 158. IVP Academic. December 6, 2022.
17 Childers, Steve. "Chinese Pastors Make Public Declaration in Face of Persecution." *The Aquila Report,* 18 Dec. 2018, theaquilareport.com/chinese-pastors-make-public-declaration-in-face-of-persecution/.
18 Maule, Will. "Persecuted Chinese Pastor Calls President Xi Jinping to Repent of His Sins." *Faithwire,* 31 Dec. 2018, www.faithwire.com/2018/12/31/persecuted-chinese-pastor-calls-president-xi-jinping-to-repent-of-his-sins/.
19 Frances made the grant of asylum public in April 2022.
20 Mahtani, Shibani. "A Student in Boston Wrote, 'I Am from Hong Kong.' an Onslaught of Chinese Anger Followed." *Boston.Com,* The Boston Globe, 28 May 2019, www.boston.com/news/local-news/2019/05/28/frances-hui-hong-kong/.
21 https://www.nytimes.com/2019/10/26/us/hong-kong-protests-colleges.html
22 Arjia Rinpoche, *Surviving the Dragon*, 34.
23 Ibid., 36.
24 Ibid., 41
25 Ibid., 44.
26 Ibid., 79.
27 Ibid., 96.
28 Ibid., 207.
29 Dhondup T. Rekjong, "Xi Jinping's War on Tibetan Buddhism," *Wall Street Journal,* November 18, 2021, https://www.wsj.com/opinion/xi-jinping-war-on-tibetan-buddhism-lanugage-china-monks-education-unity-sixth-plenum-11637269866.
30 Ibid., 217.
31 Ibid., 218.
32 His Holiness the Dalai Lama, *Voice for the Voiceless: Over Seven Decades of Struggle with China for My Land and My People* (William Morrow, 2025).
33 Frank R. Wolf with Anne Morse, *Prisoner of Conscience: One Man's Crusade for Global Human and Religious Rights* (Zondervan, 2011), 62.
34 Ibid., 123.
35 Ibid., 124.

36 Ibid., 126.
37 1 Timothy 6:10 (Amplified Bible). Words in square brackets have been omitted.
38 "Human Rights Brief." *Human Rights Brief | Washington College of Law Journals & Law Reviews | American University Washington College of Law,* digitalcommons.wcl.american.edu/hrbrief/. Accessed 2 Feb. 2026.
39 "The Economics of Organ Harvesting in China." *IRCC,* theircc.org/organharvesting/. Accessed 2 Feb. 2026
40 Ibid.
41 Feldman, Dan. "Enes Kanter's Family Disowns Him over Turkish Political Issues." *NBC Sports,* NBC Sports, 8 Aug. 2016, www.nbcsports.com/nba/news/enes-kanters-family-disowns-him-over-turkish-political-issues.
42 Mihrigul Tursun and Andrea C. Hoffmann, *Place of No Return: How I Survived China's Uyghur Camps* (Titletown Publishing, 2023), 15.
43 Ibid., 64.
44 Ibid., 64–65.
45 Ibid., 105.
46 Ibid., 119.
47 Ibid., 199.
48 Hoffman, Andrea C., et al. *Place of No Return: How I Survived China's Uyghur Camps.* Titletown Publishing, LLC, 2023. pg 163.
49 Ibid., 180.
50 Hoffman, Andrea C., et al. *Place of No Return: How I Survived China's Uyghur Camps.* Titletown Publishing, LLC, 2023. pg. 195
51 Ibid., 195.
52 Hoffman, Andrea C., et al. *Place of No Return: How I Survived China's Uyghur Camps.* Titletown Publishing, LLC, 2023. pg 198.
53 Hoffman, Andrea C., et al. *Place of No Return: How I Survived China's Uyghur Camps.* Titletown Publishing, LLC, 2023. pg 204.
54 Ibid., 195–98, 204.
55 Humanevents.com. "Ronald Reagan: We Are at War with Communists and We Must Win." *Human Events,* humanevents.com, 14 Nov. 2025, humanevents.com/2025/11/13/president-ronald-reagan-encroaching-government-controls.
56 Natan Sharansky, "Ronald Reagan: An Essay on the Legacy of an American Icon," May 14, 2025, LinkedIn, https://www.linkedin.com/pulse/natan-sharansky-ronald-reagan-essay-legacy-american-icon-cp4cc/.

ACKNOWLEDGMENTS

I MUST START BY THANKING my wife and partner in life, Mary Stauffer Brownback.

Mary's commitment to bringing out the truth, in these pages and in every other endeavor of my life, personal and professional, has been unwavering for more than forty years. The same goes for my entire family, who have been there for me every step of the way. I have been blessed in more ways than I could ever imagine. Our daughter, Liz Kutina, even had the divine inspiration for the book's cover.

I'm grateful, as well, to my assistant, Matt Goddard. Matt set up countless meetings and interviews to keep this book on track.

Peter Burns and Manus Churchill, who run the International Religious Freedom Summit I co-chair with Katrina Lantos Swett, deserve a great deal of credit. They provided insight and suggestions during the whole process. My former colleagues at the US State Department Office of International Religious Freedom, Tina Mufford, in particular, also helped form some of my thinking.

My mentor, former Congressman Frank Wolf, was supportive of my efforts from the start. I'll never forget the afternoon we spent in the cafeteria of a House office building, when he told my co-writer, Michael Arkush, and I that if we did this right, we might save lives. Michael and I were deeply moved and often referred to the conversation.

I pray Frank is right. That we do save lives.

I also want to acknowledge and thank the president of the United States, Donald J. Trump, for appointing me as the ambassador-at-large for international religious freedom in his first term and getting heartily behind the work. I am indebted, as well, to former Vice President Mike Pence and Secretary of State Mike Pompeo for their staunch global support for the cause of religious freedom.

I acknowledge the individuals and civil society groups, large and small, that have carried in their souls the yearning for religious freedom in China. These include: Bob Fu, founder of ChinaAid; Omer Kanat, executive director of the Uyghur Human Rights Project; the International Campaign for Tibet; the Falun Gong Association; Corey Jackson, founder and president of the Luke Alliance; Benedict Rogers, senior director of Fortify Rights and founder of Hong Kong Watch; and Adrian Zenz, senior fellow and director of China studies at the Victims of Communism Memorial Foundation.

Others who were very helpful include Rushan Abbas, Teng Biao, Logan Carmichael, Jeff Chen, Grace Drexel, Olivia Enos, Steven Feldstein, Scott Flipse, Ethan Gutmann, Tencho Gyatso, Arthur Herman, Elfibar Iltebir, Rana Siu Inboden, Larry Liu, Chris Meserole, Yu Ping, Lobsang Sangay, Erin Singshinsuk, Sabrina Sohail, Cynthia Sun, Tiny Tang, Ryan Xu, and Alex Zhang.

A special thanks to Anita Chang, who bailed us out on more than a few occasions with her translating skills.

This book was guided day after day by the vision and commitment of our publisher, Al Regnery of Republic Book Publishers.

Al has a long and distinguished history of bringing big problems, overlooked for years, into the spotlight. He has done it again with this project. His best idea, and there were many, was hiring Elizabeth Kantor to be our editor. Elizabeth made one superb suggestion after another. I'm also grateful to Caitlin Burdette, Katherine Ruddy, and the rest of the crew at Post Hill Press.

Michael Arkush is an incredibly accomplished writer whose skill and heart for the persecuted brought these stories to life. He was relentless. The more stories he heard, the more his blood boiled. He wants this persecution to end. His wife, Pauletta Walsh, and I worked together at the State Department in the International Religious Freedom office. She offered tremendous insights and observations along the way.

Our agent, Mel Berger of William Morris Endeavor, was invaluable from day one.

Caden Benedict and Logan Lee, students at Pepperdine University, did excellent fact checking.

Congressman Chris Smith and his current and former staff members helped enormously and were always on point on human rights issues.

I also want to thank my good friend, the best-selling author Joel Rosenberg, for writing the foreword. Joel's fictional works are prescient. His latest, *Beijing Betrayal,* alerts us about the problems ahead with China. Sadly, we are already there.

Needless to say, this book would not have been possible without the courage displayed by the people I profiled. It was a lot, maybe too much, to ask them to relive a horrible time in their lives. They are remarkable individuals. I will always pray for them and their families.

I am also deeply appreciate of everyone who has prayed for this book. For the truth to come out. Without delay. We were dependent upon their prayers.

Finally, I thank God the Father, Son, and Holy Ghost for this work that I pray brings glory to Him and frees His children to worship Him as they feel called in their hearts.

ABOUT THE AUTHORS

SAM BROWNBACK IS A DEDICATED family man and public servant. He is the only living American who has served as a Congressman, Senator, Governor, and Ambassador. Since arriving in the US Senate in 1996, he has passionately pursued religious freedom for everyone, everywhere, all the time. He is banned by the CCP from entering China due to his advocacy.

He and his wife Mary have five children and eleven grandchildren.

MICHAEL ARKUSH HAS WRITTEN OR co-written eighteen books, including bestsellers with Scottie Pippen, Phil Jackson, and Sugar Ray Leonard. A former staff writer for the *Los Angeles Times*, he has also contributed to *The New York Times* and *The Washington Post*. He lives in California with his wife, Pauletta Walsh.